S0-BWH-621

It's not me... it's you!

and
can we
NOT be friends?

laurie frankel

SOURCEBOOKS HYSTERIA™
AN IMPRINT OF SOURCEBOOKS, INC.®
NAPERVILLE, ILLINOIS

Thanks to Heather Rollins for her contribution.

Published by Sourcebooks, Inc.
P.O. Box 4410, Naperville, Illinois 60567-4410
(630) 961-3900
FAX: (630) 961-2168
www.sourcebooks.com

Library of Congress Cataloging-in-Publication Data
Frankel, Laurie
    It's not me, it's you: the modern girl's guide to breaking up/
    Laurie Frankel.
    p. cm.
    ISBN 1-887166-84-X
1. Single women—Psychology. 2. Separation (Psychology) 3. Separation (Psychology)—Humor. 4. Man-woman relationships. 5. Dating (Social customs) I. Title
    HQ800.2 .F725 2002
    306.73'4—dc21

                                                        2001007257

Printed and bound in Canada
WC 10 9 8 7 6 5 4 3 2 1

*To Alberta Rose and Gus
with abundant love
and in memory of
my sweet Disco.*

Contents

Introduction vii

Section I: You Are Woman. Hear Yourself Roar! 1

Chapter 1 Emergency Broadcast System:
A Story about Getting Dumped................. 3

Chapter 2 Who Unplugged the Mojo?: Exploring
the Southern-Most Hemisphere............... 23

Chapter 3 Universal Truths to Ponder:
Just Like It Sounds, Only Better 31

Chapter 4 The Five Stages of Being Single (Again):
Be a "Been There, Done That" Master......... 63

Chapter 5 Finding Mr. Produce: Love's Potential
among the Fruits and Vegetables............. 77

Chapter 6 Over My Dead Body or Aided-Dating
Methods 101: A Worldwide Web of Men Awaits! . 85

Section II: Ex Files 107

Chapter 7 Ex Sex: Need I Say More?................. 109

Chapter 8 Ex Ex: A Not-So-Merry Go-Round
with Past Loves 121

Chapter 9 Ex Engaged: HE's moved on to Ruin
Someone Else's Life...Forever 133

Chapter 10 Pre Ex: Selling Your "Previously
Owned" Boyfriend 145

Chapter 11 Never Ex: A Fake Boyfriend Is a Must-Have. . . . 155

Chapter 12 Life After Ex: The Care and Feeding of Your
New Pet Boyfriend 165

Section III: The End. 175

Chapter 13 What to Expect When You're Least
Expecting: A Counterintuitive Commitment
to One's Singlehood. 177

Introduction

think of this book as a hot, steamy bowl of ibuprofen soup for the single soul, just like over-the-counter Grandma used to make. It picks up where weary friends fall asleep and offers temporary relief from the major aches and pains associated with being single: blind dates, getting dumped, and having to tell your mother that, yes, you know a dog is not a replacement for a man. Imagine getting all that without any of the potentially cancerous, saccharin aftertaste commonly associated with other "soulful" books.

This book is your 24 x 365 portable pocket pal for those times (read: period) when you temporarily "lose perspective":

> Nobody loves me.
> Everybody hates me.
> Guess I'll go eat worms...

Sound familiar? We've all been there. Yes, even the girl with the perfect hair and flawless manicure you see riding the subway every day to work. She, too, is an occasional worm-eater. So, the next time you find yourself reaching for yet another heaping serving of slime-under-glass, reach for this book instead. Guaranteed to satisfy or your worms back!

Interspersed throughout are Q&A-format questions from Laurie's LoveLogic™. At Laurie's LoveLogic you can get answers to nagging love questions, read answers to questions you're too afraid to ask, or just plain feel better about yourself by reading about other people's horrible situations! The questions are real. The responses are real. My front teeth are not (broke them off on a table in the fourth grade).

I'll also share with you six incredible (but true!) over-the-top "Ex-Rated" date stories designed to make you feel better about the current state of your singlehood and/or dating affairs, should they be less than stellar. So you've dated a few freaks. Think you're special? Think again.

Why read this book? Because relationships, like periods, have a cycle: it's called "before," "during," and "after" (also known as forever...). This genetically fueled, species-promoting, cyclical yearning starts at age thirteen and, if we're at all lucky, ends at death. "Before" and "after" is where this book comes in handy. To stay healthy and well-nourished during these unattached stages, women need a heaping serving of not-for-dummies, cutesy-free humor with a side of sisterhood understanding smothered in yeah-it-sucks gravy.

Read this book if:

___You're single.

___You're single and it occasionally sucks.

___You're single, it occasionally sucks, and you find laughter is the best medicine.

___You're single, it occasionally sucks, and you find laughter at other people's horrible situations somehow comforting in a morbid way you would never want to admit in public.

Well, if you're single, you've come to the right place—especially those of you who agreed with, but were too embarrassed to check, the last box. (We know who you are because, on certain bad days, it's all of us.) Enjoy!

You Are Woman, Hear Yourself ROAR!

The point of this section is best summed up
by a bumper sticker I saw on the back
of a car in Boy's Town in Chicago:

The Queen Goddess
respectfully requests
that you please
BE FABULOUS!

—one—

Emergency Broadcast System:

a Story about Getting Dumped

The signal you have just heard...

Collapse unexpectedly onto the kitchen floor. Lie there. Don't move. Don't try to get up. You may injure yourself further. And wait. Just lie there and wait until someone comes to help even if you live alone. While it is true no one will really come, if you pretend, you can rest a while.

Melt. Melt into the floor. Get comfortable. Find a comfortable position on the hardwood floor. If you collapse in one of your carpeted rooms, so much the better—lucky you. Don't cheat and roll to a carpeted area—that just ruins the moment.

Sink. Sink way down. Picture the world as black. Hate all your friends. Even the ones who may be coming over to help. Hate all your coupled friends and especially hate engaged girlfriends who hold their ring fingers up and say, "My shiny ring!"

If you have a pet, now would be a good time to hunt it down and squeeze it. After all those 4:00 AM walks and foreign-object-ingested vet bills, it owes you. Track it down and, if you can, curl up with it on your bed. Don't worry about missing out on your floor moment—you have, at minimum, a two-month future of falling onto the floor to look forward to.

Hug the dog. (If all you have is a cat, hug the cat.) When it struggles to leave to do its own thing, wrap its head and forelegs in a half nelson and call it a day. If it continues to struggle, try a full.

Weep. Then bawl directly into the fur of the animal you are holding. (Get snotty about it. Do not concern yourself with etiquette. Don't forget with whom you are dealing—many animals eat ca-ca and call it dessert.) Realize the animal you have loved with all your heart and soul will not necessarily recognize the hiccuping and snot-filled howlings of your broken heart. Hope they will. Keep practicing your full nelson.

Cry so hard you temporarily cry yourself out. Make a few manufactured crying sounds to encourage another round to make sure you are really tapped out, then let it go. Enjoy, sort of, the fact that because you now feel nothing, you think you're feeling better. And let that sweet and nebulous thought carry you off into the dreamless sleep of the dead.

Sleep. Feel like a two-ton bar of iron ore sinking to the bottom of Lake Michigan because that's where you're going. Straight to the bottom. Sink past the Pabst Blue Ribbon bottles. Settle into the back seat of a 1962 baby blue Pontiac Le Mans.

Fight the free fall for six weeks. If you are one of those people who learns things by reading them, go ahead and take the accelerated route and proceed directly to the bottom. However, if you are one of those "that's-not-me" people, engage the struggle and feel humbled when it proves true after all.

Wake from your leaden sleep feeling unsurprisingly unrefreshed. Get up to face the day. Shower. Reward your efforts by pretending it's nighttime all over again, knowing that by the time you wake, it really will be.

If this had been an actual emergency...

Wake up again, this time with your head the size and consistency of way over-boiled cauliflower. Get up to pee. Shuffle down the hall exaggerating your dragging footsteps. Lose your balance. Catch yourself on the wall beside the linen closet. Think how pathetic you look.

Pee and wipe yourself and worry that's the only foreign object that will ever touch you down there again. Burst into tears right on the toilet. Heave. Carelessly reach behind you for the box of Kleenex on the toilet tank lid. Knock over a bottle of hair mousse and Stridex pads. Startle the dog.

Swear. Swear again. Swear until the words don't make sense anymore. And then giggle. Giggle like this until you worry you may be losing it.

Worry you're losing it and think who you should call before you do. Think about calling Him. (No, not your maker. Your ex.) Yearn for it. Secrete it. Manufacture it like an enzyme you need to survive. Dial his digits. Hang up before it has a chance to ring. Remember he has caller ID. Panic. Cry. Puke. Repeat.

Put on makeup and know you still look like a "before" picture. Think: "No wonder he left me." Look into the mirror and say, "Why did you leave me?" in a high, tinny voice. Fall to the floor again. Did you remember to grab your pet? Call your pet again and again. Think: "Even my _____ (cat/dog/ferret/etc.) hates me." Wail. Let the machine pick up. Wonder if it's him. Know it's not, but still hope.

Call your mom. Call your mom. Call your mom. Cry like a little girl. Call your mom and cry like the little girl you once were. Let her offer to come visit. Call her the next day and tell her it's not necessary.

Do things you and he enjoyed together...alone. Get weepy and cranky. Hide. Don't return phone calls. Disappear from Earth. Discover Atlantis and stay there.

You would have been notified...

Walk as if you've just had surgery...down there. Gingerly toe the road and the sidewalk. Drive slowly, just like your grandmother (not fast, like mine). Experience turning left. Talk carefully and laminate your thoughts. Feel what it's like to be stupid.

Do a friend review. See who's there for you and who says the exact right thing. See who takes your call at 2:00 AM and who lets the machine get it. Send sweet, sappy notes to those who do. Cry tears of joy that you have friends like these. Eliminate the ones who took call-waiting while you cried. Jot down the names and email addresses of friends who, two weeks after the break-up, stopped asking how you were doing. Put their names on every online junk mail list you can find.

Roll tape on all the fun things you and your ex used to do together. Torture yourself with bed-and-breakfast memories. Wonder if his parents miss you.

- ❋ Spoon your dog and wonder if you're sick.
- ❋ Still sleep on your side of the bed.
- ❋ Pretend to feel your biological clock ticking.
- ❋ Wonder what it'll be like to grow old. Alone.

Bake another batch of double-chocolate, chocolate chip cookies. Watch back-to-back reruns of *Melrose Place*. Envy Heather Locklear as her character and as herself. Know that if your genes had lined up like a grown-up version of Baby Sunshine, you wouldn't be home watching *Melrose Place* (but you'd still be eating chocolate chip cookies). Force yourself to sit through the entire hour. Pretend that in the future, when you're better, you'll purposely schedule social engagements around *Melrose Place*.

Look in the mirror and deride yourself. Dye your gray for the first time. Notice crow's feet around your nose. Get a two hundred dollar makeover. Return everything you bought the following week. Ignore the dirty looks the saleslady gives you as she rings you out. Tell yourself you're prettier than she is. Smile.

Get really grungy. Let the oil on your scalp build up to the point where your hair looks as if it were naturally straight. Notice you have B.O. Go without a shower one half-day longer than you think you can stand. Shower extra long, feel refreshed. Know your friends appreciated the thirty minutes their phone did not ring.

Look at your body after showering. Glance down there. Say, "Hiya, pink pal." Whisper, "Hey, snapless snapper." Ask, "What up, hoochie coo?" Feel deafened by the silence that follows. Wonder if "it" has been permanently disconnected. Think about developing a body of work you can throw yourself into. Call for cable.

If you get dumped around spring, combine it with a spring cleaning. If it's December, clean anyway. Send your dust bunnies to *The Guinness Book of World Records*. Give away the dress he bought that made you look like Mrs. Butterworth. Throw away the Snapple, 100 percent bran, and Jif Extra Crunchy you'd thoughtfully purchased just for him.

Get wicked drunk. Go on that forty dollar, open-bar booze cruise. Keep your vodka grapefruit in one hand and your beer chaser in the other. Talk to everyone you don't know. Go to the side of the boat and have a quiet moment with yourself. (Not that kind.) Wander off to find the bathroom and see a couple kissing out of the corner of your eye. Slow down and observe them like an alien. Wonder if you're a pervert. Get morose. Knock back your watered-down Greyhound and chug the flat beer. Continue looking for the bathroom and wish your ex were there to take you home, give you aspirin, and tuck you in. Cry. Pee. Repeat. Forget to wipe your runny mascara.

We now return you to your regularly scheduled program.

Read the personals over a bowl of Honey Nut Cheerios. Feel pathetic that you're thinking of placing a personal ad. Place one. Win ad-of-the-week. Get a dozen free roses. Tell only your mother because you are too embarrassed otherwise. Meet lots of losers. Begin to see the not-so-unique qualities of your ex...in everyone. Find out your mother and your aunt thought he was a jerk.

Indulge yourself with pedicures and facials. Buy those faux-suede, zip-up-the-back brown pants you've had your eye on. Do it. Do it. Do it. Don thong underwear when you wear them. Tell the world to watch out. Take the thong off in the bar bathroom and flush it down the toilet. Vow never to wear one again.

Feel good about yourself and worry it won't last. Worry you'll feel crappy again too soon. Feel crappy again. Feel good about feeling crappy again so you can stop worrying.

Drop a glass and realize you're down to two. Remember him telling you you needed new glasses and silverware and plates and you should organize your pantry better and eat more fiber and conserve water when doing the dishes and dye your hair red and laugh more quietly and think more softly. Remember he never told you you were beautiful.

Bake. Bake a pie using only fresh strawberries, raspberries, lemon juice, and sugar. Buy the crust. Eat it hot with Breyer's Vanilla Bean all-natural ice cream every day after lunch and dinner until it is gone. Bake another.

Wake up and think of the dream you were having. Kiss the dog good morning. Snuggle under your comforter for five more minutes of sleep. Remember you are single and have been dumped. Think how that was not the first thing you thought of upon waking. Know you're making progress. Feel a little sad.

Talk to your dog deeply and philosophically. Know he doesn't understand you. Keep talking. Throw the kong. Chase it since your dog won't. Realize you mistook crumbs for love.

Get the unabridged version of *Grimm's Fairy Tales* and read them aloud to yourself. Smile. Get up early. Go to the park with the dog at 6:00 AM. See the lake crashing over the sea wall. Feel the spray on your face. Witness a rainbow. Enjoy how incredibly beautiful the world is.

Find an old picture of the two of you arm-in-arm. Notice how sexy you are. And that he doesn't look so cute. Be glad that someone other than yourself is now holding his whining hand. Know you deserve better. Hope it's out there. Live your days as if it is. Love yourself even though it seems like it isn't.

Man of His Word

Dear Laurie

I have been divorced for sixteen years and am starting to date again at the age of forty. My question is this: At what point should I tell my WHITE boyfriend that my ex-husband was BLACK? I am an ASIAN-PACIFIC ISLANDER. I have not been serious with anyone since the failed marriage and am not even sure how to deal with the situation. For me, race is not an issue, but I don't know when to reveal that part of my past. Any input would help. Thanks.

Me, unsure of next step

Dear "Unsure ASIAN-PACIFIC ISLANDER,"

Sixteen years! Wow, welcome back! I took three off at one point and, upon re-entry, felt like the robot character in *Sleeper*. One thing always to keep in mind (and something you may have gathered from reading this column): everyone's messed up in their own special way. No one has all the answers and very few really have it together, so whatever funkadelia you're feeling about being in a relationship again, your WHITE boyfriend is probably feeling it double.

Your question: "At what point should I tell my WHITE boyfriend my ex-husband was BLACK?"

Now. Yesterday. When you first began having the feeling you wanted to tell your WHITE boyfriend your ex was BLACK. More importantly: when you first began worrying if you told your WHITE boyfriend about your BLACK ex he would leave you.

Hmmm? I thought so. I mean, why else would this be an issue for you? Who cares that your ex was BLACK? You're an ASIAN-PACIFIC ISLANDER (congratulations). I happen to be WHITE. Some of my best friends are...

As your current lover, I'd care more—much more—if your ex was some sort of abusive, creepy loser, a pimp who dressed poorly, or a close friend of Tony Soprano. If your current beau is going to dump you over, or is freaked out by, the fact that your previous husband was BLACK, wouldn't you rather know that sooner than later? Wouldn't you want to know so you could send him packing with his other skinhead brethren in northern Idaho? Why, yes, you would!

Anytime you're ashamed/embarrassed/afraid to divulge personal information to a significant other, well, by golly, that's the time divulgification (yes, I made that up) is most necessary. A life lived in fear—and roads not taken—is no life at all. Instead, it's an insidious form of settling and compromise in the most negative sense.

The not-so-short answer: Where to find the courage to face your fears? Deep inside. (Play New Age music here please.) I'M

SERIOUS. (Don't whisper that one.) You've got to have high-minded, personal convictions and a strong realistic sense of self to make it in this world. Once you have an inkling about all that, you've got to protect it, which means standing up for your beliefs and surrounding yourself with good-hearted souls.

What a nice surprise it will be when you finally get this concern off your PAN-ASIAN chest and find out that your WHITE boyfriend couldn't give a rat's patootie your ex was BLACK. You find out he loves you for you; your feelings for each other deepen; you thank God you're no longer single; and you live happily ever after (play Mac Davis's "Having my Baby" here).

Sound of needle scratching on record or CD player falling to ground: And, if not? Should WHITE boyfriend prove to be the narrow-minded racist lout you pegged him for? Alas, curl up on your kitchen floor with Al Green for a few weeks and call it a day (for those born after 1980, substitute Macy Gray).

Lovingly&logically yours,
Laurie

Couple Achieves Child:
Story at Eleven

Dear Laurie,

My boyfriend and I broke up two months ago from a three-year relationship. Within that time, we achieved a son and a mortgage payment (I know—what were we thinking?). We were engaged and going to be married. Things just never worked out that way. Anyway, neither of us can afford to keep the house on our own and neither of us can stand the thought of being apart from our son.

So, for the past two months, we have been living in the house together, which is very uncomfortable for me since I am getting on with my life and he wants to recreate the past. He knows I don't want to get back together, but I don't think he really cares about me. It has always been about him in the past, I mean, why should it be different now? So, my question is, how do I handle the situation of telling him I need to get away from him without him thinking I'm some conniver who just had a kid to get child support from him? He has stated to me that that is what he thinks I did. The fact that he's known me for three years has escaped his memory since the break-up.

Woeful in Wisconsin

Whoa, whoa, whoa, Wisconsin, you've gotten yourself in quite the jam here! My, my. Hmmm, okay, first, I'm sorry. Really, I am. This is all very hard and unfortunate. Okay, group hug is over. Now, let's move on to solving the pickle you've gotten yourself into.

You say, "We were engaged and were going to be married. Things just never worked out that way." Things just never worked out that way? Hello?! Woeful, repeat after me: "My boyfriend and I chose not to get married. For a variety of complex and not completely understood reasons it was a willful decision made by two adults of sane mind." Got it? Alrighty then. Moving right along.

Now's as good a time as any for my diatribe on why the institution of marriage exists in the first place—it forces people to try a little harder (like Avis). It's my unprofessional opinion that every couple comes to a point where they want to head for the hills (in varying degrees). Couples who have made the matrimonial commitment (i.e., had friends/family witness the union, ponied up a lot of money for the gathering, made their friends wear ugly dresses in public, gotten a piece of paper and a stupid video to show for it) are forced to reconsider the hill-fleeing idea a little longer than most. Now, I especially think second thoughts are in order when you've "achieved" a child (Merriam-Webster: achieve 2. "to get or attain as the result of exertion")—by golly, I guess you did indeed "achieve" your son.

You say, "My boyfriend and I broke up two months ago... He knows I don't want to get back together but I don't think he really cares about me."

I sense a bit of ambivalence here on your part. If you thought he really cared about you, would you want to get back together with him? In other words, is your wanting to be with him contingent on how you want him to feel about you? (How old are you all anyway? Just wondering.) How do you feel? What do you want (independent of how you want him to feel)?

About the we-already-broke-up thing, I'm of two minds. My first mind says: Once broken up, always broken up—you broke up for a reason. Move on. But the kid thing complicates the picture a little, so...

First mind with kid caveat: You brought a kid into the world! Think really long and really hard and see if you can make amends. Don't stay together for the sake of the child (you'll end up teaching him that love is a farce—baaaaad). What I am saying is take the time to see if you still have love for this rat man you once cooed over. If you do, go get yourselves a great shrink, commit to doing some serious, hard work, and prepare to grow, grow, grow as individuals, as a partnership, as a family, but hopefully not to a bigger dress or suit size.

If, on the other hand, after long bouts of hand-wringing, the love is gone—truly, truly gone—bite the bullet, bid each other *adieu*, and get yourselves a dashing set of his-and-her lawyers. If you're over him like you say you are (unconvincingly, I might add), what do you care if he thinks you're "a conniver"?

The short answer: Time for each of you to attend remedial adult classes and learn to be one. This is your beautiful house. And you've made a kid together. Maybe the love is gone—maybe not. Find out, make some thoughtful decisions, and grow up!

Lovingly&logically yours,
Laurie

Dear Laurie:

I just turned thirty, am pretty, smart, athletic, funny...I have a great group of friends, a very cool dog, and live in a big city. I am cultured, well-educated, and love, I mean like, my job. Aside from the occasional bad hair day or zit (still, at thirty!) life is pretty good. The problem is I can't believe, am incredibly disappointed about, feel it is supremely unfair that, I have not yet met the man of my dreams. I hate to admit it, but with increasing frequency I am beginning to think it's never going to happen. In fact, at times I am downright despondent. Words of wisdom, please.

Verveless in Vermont

Dear V.V.:

When the going gets tough, I thought Vermonters go cow-tipping. What's the matter—off season? Oh, easy now, some of my best friends eat Ben & Jerry's, so lighten up.

Okay, down to business. Yeah, it sucks not to have a companion. Seriously, it really does—am I helping? When you're single, it's like someone turned down the hue and tint buttons on your Sony Trinitron. The picture's not as bright or beautiful, but before you go getting all maudlin on me (I was trying to work "maudlin" into this column, so thank you), let's get some perspective.

To give the illusion of perspective, you draw a horizon line and a vanishing point. This helps bring your basic fruit and flower arrangement to life (if you're Dutch, you throw in a dead bird for good measure). The horizon line is the faraway thing that grounds you spatially. It helps you see the bigger picture, regardless of the immediate content, which can change until the balance is right (many artists drew over parts of paintings that didn't work for them, just as one may dispose of a not-quite-right man...or men). Then there's the vanishing point, which focuses the eye on the picture prize. Translated, that means in spite of past disappointments, you continue to have hope you will get what you want in life. And if you don't, there's always the option of cutting off a piece of your ear and going crazy!

Is this all too artsy-fartsy for you? Well then, how about considering the wisdom of the ever-relevant phrase, "Keep breathing!" That's what my mom says and it helps because otherwise you turn blue and appear very unattractive (no man would want you then). In other words, keep doing the things that bring you joy.

In the meantime, maybe the doofus you've been flirting with on your volleyball team or that hipster who eyes you on the bus every day will wake up, smell the caffeine, and finally ask you out (or maybe you'll screw up the courage and ask him out!). And while you are busy being joyous, don't forget to tell your friends you are "in the market" (because one out of every four hundred and fifty million marriages results from getting set up...).

The short answer: Hang in there, girl, because what you want will happen. In the meantime, enjoy life, have a pint of New York Super Fudge Chunk, and leave all standing cows alone.

Lovingly&logically yours,
Laurie

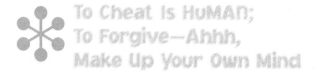

To Cheat Is HuMAN; To Forgive—Ahhh, Make Up Your Own Mind

Dear Laurie:

Why do married men have affairs?

Thanks, Gina

Dear Gina:

Oh, Gina! Crazy Gina. Silly Gina. Am I correct in assuming your married man is having an affair on you or is this just a rhetorical question? If I am correct, my knee-jerk response would be dump the fat slob. Then again, I know there are two sides to every story and so we shall proceed.

Considering the male biology—the fact that they are mechanically designed to impregnate the world from age twelve 'til death, while we females gestate for nine months at a pop during our thirty-year viability window—I think the real question here is: Why don't more married men have affairs? Yes? Agreed? In fact, why are men faithful at all?

When I listen to my male friends (and I think this means I probably need to get a brand spanking new set o' male friends), in an ideal world they would be doing "it" with as many women in as many Kama-Sutric positions as (physically) possible with the most minimal amount of downtime for eating and making a living. In my "professional" opinion, if men could, many would like their personal black books at least the size of a large metropolitan area's white pages minus the front government and city/county sections.

"But Laurie," you say, "what about true love and getting swept off our collective feet by Prince Charming and living happily ever after, etc., etc.?" Long live fantasy and hope and slightly modified fairy tales, girlfriends, is what I say!! Not all men are cheaters, but the ones who are give everyone else a bad name!

Yeah, not all men are sniff doggy dogs, skank monsters, slow-shuffling, one-eyed sloths—no siree Bobitt. But, for those of you blessed with one, well, I think Nancy Sinatra summed it up nicely when she sang that killer tune of hers, "These Boots Were Made for Walkin'."

Personally, infidelity is one of my nonnegotiables, with mitigating circumstance playing about a .001 percent role in the decision-making process. But Gina, only you can decide for yourself why your or your friend's man cheated and if you or said friend can live with this type of behavior in a mate.

I didn't really answer your question, did I? Okay.

The short answer: Men cheat because they can, often because there is a problem at home with which they are too chicken—I mean emotionally ill-equipped—to deal. They go elsewhere to find temporary solace/relief.

From high atop my soapbox, I would like to say I am a big proponent of finishing dinner before starting on dessert. And for the cheaters in the audience, I have twenty words: if he/she cheated to be with you, eventually he/she will cheat on you to be with somebody else. Ahh, the circle of life....

Lovingly&logically yours,
Laurie

two

Who Unplugged the Mojo?

Exploring the Southern-Most Hemisphere

for those times when you can hardly get the motor idling—let alone running—I find working a little haiku into your routine can do wonders. As told to me by, uh, a good friend:

Several long months
(Or days) have passed
Since you've felt the call.

(In mojo matters,
"Long" is a relative term,
Don't you know, sister.)

A hottie smiles at you
From the cover of GQ
At the grocery check-out.

Did I say hottie?
I meant HOTTIE with cap "H".
Caution: Very Hot!

Imagine dining
By candlelight with champagne.
Dessert anyone?

Oo, oh, ahh...uh oh.
Thoughts of unpaid bills appear,
And unreturned calls.

"Paper or plastic?"
Jolts you from your reverie.
You say, "Brought my own."

Your eye drifts back
To the hottie in the mag.
"Now just where were we?"

Approaching dessert!
Ooey, gooey, rich and ch...
Yeah, whatever—yawn.

What? How can that be?
Then the sad truth dawns on you.
It all makes sense now.

Unbeknownst to you,
The mojo has been unplugged.
Finito. Kaput.

Home improvement time.
Hey, Martha Stewart!
"Year's subscription, please."

Beaujolais

God Has Left the Building and Entered the Internet

> Dear Laurie,
>
> How do you get more people interested in living for Jesus Christ?
>
> Jets

So, there I am—waiting for that special question to come across my emailbox (of course, all questions I receive are special because each and everyone one of you is special...). But, as I was saying, there I am waiting for that *really* special question, the one that *speaks* to me, and then, like a flash of light, there it was from "Jets": "How do you get more people interested in living for Jesus Christ?"

I'd been meaning to work religion into a column answer and just hadn't yet found the right segue. Now, like manna from heaven, serendipity, synchronicity, here it is. First, let me point out that I am not a religious woman, but I am also no atheist. I *do* believe there is something going on here that's bigger than the both of us. But since every time I open a newspaper or turn on the radio one devout religious group is slaying an opposing devout religious group, I now say: down with organized crime—I mean religion. Yeah, yeah, I accept and respect each and every one of you in your unique-but-different wholenesses—it's just that license-to-kill part I have a hard time with.

Now, on with the question. At first read I saw: "How do you get more people living for Jesus Christ?" as in, how does one get all the other ones to sing the praises of J.C., the long-haired, skinny One? Then I thought, no, maybe Jets is punctuationally challenged and really meant: "How do you get more people living, for Jesus Christ," as in, goddammit folks, live it up already!

See the power of the comma in that last interpretation? You know? And all of this reminded me of a particularly impactful teaching movie I was shown in Mrs. Smith's third-grade class, *Punctuation: The Forgotten Language.* A boy and a girl were working on a project together:

Girl: You don't mind working on the project now?
Boy: No I don't, want to do it now?

But with a simple slip of that gosh-darn comma, the boy turns into the stubborn, surly type all you women write in to me about and the scenario takes a decidedly negative turn:

Boy: No, I don't want to do it now.

Hunh! I know some of you out there are gasping as you read this, thinking: Oh, that Laurie! She's so harsh, so irreverent, so rude—her poor mother! But you're also the ones who secretly listen to Howard Stern and then publicly poo-poo him when making polite party conversation. Besides, what does Jets take me for, the Messiah?

How does this all relate to things lover-ly and logical, you ask? Well, the short answer might be: It really doesn't. But the even shorter answer might be: Who cares?

Lovingly&logically yours,
Laurie

If You Can't Be with the One You Love, Honey...Cry

Dear Laurie,

When the one you love never wants to make love, what do you do?

Cry. You read that right. First you need to cry and feel bad about your situation because it is sad. As you can see, your question is one of the shorter ones I've received, so there's a lot of guesswork to be done.

I feel like a broken record, but here goes. Sex is one of the great perks of being in a relationship. It's an aspect that makes a two-person union unique. When lovers stop loving, it's an indication of a change in the relationship which can either be addressed and repaired, addressed and abandoned, never addressed and become increasingly dysfunctional, or never addressed and increasingly functional for the two participating dysfunctionals. I'm all about addressing big elephants in the living room and especially those in the bedroom. Unless you have a particularly big bedroom, they inevitably get in the way.

The short answer: So, honey, time to ask your mate the sixty-four-thousand dollar question: Why don't you want to make love with me anymore? GULP—what a scary question. Yes, I know, but a life lived in fear is no life at all. Remember, had you truly wanted to stay under your rock, you wouldn't have written in. Good luck.

Lovingly&logically yours,
Laurie

Tomato

three

Universal Truths to Ponder:

Just Like It Sounds, Only Better

In no particular order:

Boring men do not get less boring over time.

They may become less poor or have less hair, but they do not get less boring. Boring people, in fact, have a great—sometimes limitless—capacity to become more boring. When in the throes of severe loneliness, datelessness, and long bouts of "dinner for one," it's easy to ignore this primary law of personality physics: boring bodies at rest stay at boring rest.

Corollary: Boring people can temporarily become less boring over beer.

Yours. But rest assured that in the time it takes for your beer goggles to wear off, these boring souls will revert back to their natural state. Boring people also can be perceived as less boring when other, more boring options are present (in other words: when you've had a slew of rotten dates). And remember, just because a typically boring person cracks an intelligent joke once a quarter, it doesn't mean you initially misjudged and they are truly fascinating. It means you're drinking beer again.

Opposites attract for sixty days and then they expire.

Mates look and act like each other for a reason. People like, or are comfortable with, themselves. And when you're comfortable while on a date, you're less likely to say, "Would you look at her? They must be fake," or "I love Air Supply!" So, short of cloning, what could be better than having more of yourself around?

Corollary: Like-minded souls travel in packs.

Simply put, losers attract losers (and cool people attract cool people), so the next time you have a lousy date and your mother says, "Maybe he has friends," tell her you're sure he does and ask for a moment of silence to mourn the sad fact that you'll probably end up dating all of them.

Caveat to the Corollary: Cool people occasionally spring from loser families and vicey versee.

So, you've met the man of your dreams and can't wait to meet his dream family. Hold it right there, dreamer (sound of CD skipping for those too young to know what vinyl is). Since we can't choose our families, having harmonious (or humanoid) familial relations is a crapshoot (which is why writing "dysfunctional family" is redundant, while writing "functional family" is not). Good luck at shooting them craps.

Familiarize yourself with the four seasons of man.

Before committing to 'til-death-do-us-part, make sure you've gone through at least four seasons with your future betrothed. Four seasons allows you to see one's entire wardrobe—no nasty fashion surprises—among other things.

Corollary: Beware of males wearing spandex.

When a new biking date shows up in lycra-wear showcasing a variety of skinny legs, politely avert your eyes and make a mental note to become permanently unavailable. There's no need to overshare on a first date. Leave that for date two....

Looks matter more in terms of indescribable chemistry than standard degrees of beauty.

Whoever told you they didn't was either lying, was your mother, or was named Mrs. Macleay, my fourth-grade teacher, who upon seeing me after I accidentally broke off my two front teeth told me beauty was on the inside.

Corollary: When on a date, check others out discreetly, using the "polite swivel" setting.

It is human nature to admire beauty. What do you think drew you to bed each other in the first place? But whiplash-style rubber-necking in front of your mate is intensely rude. Please, gawk compassionately.

Corollary Encore: If you look like shit, you'll run into your ex.

Don't walk around looking like shit. The benefits are three-fold: it keeps you from seeing your ex, you generally feel better about yourself, and you look fabulous for snagging new dudes.

Blinded by the lack of light, or the benefit of the brainy doubt.

When you are with a weak-minded, beautiful person, it takes, on average, two-and-a-half times longer to realize they are mental dwarfs than were you with an average-looking person. The reason for this is simple: appreciating beauty activates the high-energy mojo center, forcing the evaluation-processing switchboard to run on a poorly configured back-up generator. The resulting output is inconclusive at best. For more reliable data, cross your legs and compute again.

Corollary: The brain/body compromise, or the 80/20 rule of social economics.

No woman really wants to marry a super-hottie-patottie because that much eye candy could give a girl one mean cavity in her life. And no woman really wants to marry a total brain trust either because that could make her Sleeping Beauty (sans the beauty part). What does a woman want and need? The brain/body compromise! Just enough titillation down below to get the party started (that's the 20 percent) and then a great deal more upstairs to keep the music flowin' 'til the wee hours (that's the 80 percent). Rock on!

Asking a guy out is like acting every part in a play.

Great for putting on a one-woman show. Not great for much else. As much as men say they'd love a woman to ask them out, the truth is they don't understand the question. Guys would love a woman to ask them out in their fantasies, but in reality, they "go nervous," feel unmanly, and wonder what other roles this date-askin,' Xena-warrior woman is going to take over next.

Corollary: Guys need skywriting-sized hints in order to feel comfortable enough to ask a woman out.

Rejected by girls since birth, guys are wounded, weary, shell-shocked soldiers. If you like one, take pity and draw him a chart.

Beware of forty-year-old men who never married.

Not to be totally sexist, but in our society, in general, men do the asking. Men pull the trigger. As non-trigger-pulling men age, the enzyme that once would have allowed them to bust a move gets used up or atrophies or something. These men are therefore less and less likely, maybe even less capable, to do the commitment hustle. Older, commitment-phobic men emit many early warning signs (inattentive, uncaring behavior you find yourself repeatedly rationalizing away). Watch out for them and don't make me say, "I told you so."

Corollary: Nice guys finish last.

Bad guys finish second-to-last, while thoughtful guys with passionate interests and a spine finish first. I'm looking to snag myself one of them thar thoughtful guys—only one to a customer, please.

People who have bad breath don't know they have bad breath.

If they did, why would they keep subjecting you to it? And while it's hard to tell them, tell them! Offer up a piece of gum, perhaps a mint, every time you see them (the same theory applies to B.O., only a stick of gum will prove less effective). Should they refuse your offerings, try leaning back when they lean in. Grimace, hack, and cough if necessary. Wave your hand in front of your face as if staving off cancerous smoke rings. Do whatever it takes—the proliferation of the human race depends on you.

Corollary: You cannot change people.

Stick with your underwear. Men are sold "as is." No exchanges (unless you get a divorce). No refunds (unless you get a great attorney). A perfect guy who is only a teeny bit narcissistic, yells only on special occasions, or has just the slightest methamphetamine habit, ain't perfect. When one of these specimens appears on the end of your line, strongly clear your throat and say, "Go fish."

Never make an important decision while on your period.

Never do anything on your period, for that matter. Simply eat bon bons and contemplate life until the coast is clear. Men, were they to get them, would make periods a monthly national holiday.

Corollary: When in doubt, eat chocolate— the good kind and lots of it.

Don't worry about the calories. Worry about the loved ones whose heads you'll rip off if you skip your prescribed dose.

Caveat to the Corollary: Never ask if something makes your butt look big.

Unless you have skewed anorexic vision, you know damn well if your butt is big. If it's big and you're okay with that, more power to you! If it's big and you're not okay with it, then do something about it. (Did you know actively pursuing your dreams gives you carte blanche to bitch? Yes, it's true!) Should someone corner you and ask, in your professional butt opinion, does their butt look big, don't answer. Say instead, "How about them (place local sports team name here)?"

Caveat to the Caveat: Don't wear a thong in public.

Is it hidden underneath a skirt or a pair of pants? Wear it 'til the cows come home (wear it even if the livestock are a no-show). But if it's just you, your thong, and a gentle beach breeze,

DON'T DO IT. I don't care how pristine your tush is either, how fabulously air-brushed you've managed to make it appear, how Nair barely-there hairless it is. Some things are better left to the imagination and your bungy-hole cover is one of them. I can't even believe we need to have this discussion!

Dating is not fair.

Dating is a struggle. Dating is hard. Occasionally, it has clear-sky potential and feels scrubbed clean. Then it goes back to being hard and not fair. This is the reason why people get married—they are taking a time-out from dating.

Corollary: A couple is better than a single.

Societally speaking, when you're part of a couple, no matter how dysfunctional, you look more normal than if you're single (and it makes seating arrangements at dinner parties so much more...symmetrical).

The More Corollaries the Merrier: Never say the word "spinster"—even in jest.

It's bad ju ju incarnate. "Bachelor" is to Godiva chocolate as "spinster" is to hot-and-rotting cottage cheese. I cast an evil eye on its etymologist. Shame, shame, shame on him and his mother.

If someone sets you up on a blind date, you are not a loser.

You may feel like a loser, but you are not. In fact, you are lucky. You are lucky to have friends setting up your single ass. When your ass is no longer single, return the favor to other single asses (provided they're not truly asses).

Corollary: "Maybe you're too picky" is a pointless and almost always rhetorical comment.

Perhaps you are, but the fact remains you still don't like the guy you don't want to be with. (Note to family/friends: stop saying this.)

Do unto others as you would have those higher on the food chain do unto you.

In other words, you never know who knows whom. Should someone be kind enough to try and "elevate" you from the realm of singlehood to doublehood, be gracious. Be thankful and courteous. If you have a tendency to be a wench bag and word gets out, good luck ever dating in your town again (which could be a plus, depending on your town). Along the lines of sharing your gum in grade school, this truth goes a long way toward encouraging social harmony and getting yourself invited to your neighbor's see-and-be-seen party.

Corollary: Do unto man as you would an aluminum can. Recycle him!

Recycled material is material transformed into something different from its initially intended use. Recycled men are men with potential but poor cosmic timing. Say you meet a guy and, for whatever reason (he lives five hundred miles away...in a Yurt or still walks on all fours), romantic timing is catastrophically wrong, but platonic timing is supernaturally right. Time to reduce and reuse, girls! If you find his wit astronomically enjoyable, enjoy it. If his outdoorsy nature suits you, wear it. Should his stellar brain activity rock your world, rock on. Because some day things may change. He could move and sell his Yurt or begin walking upright. You could start viewing him in a different light. One thing could lead to another and before you know it, you're wondering: boxers or tightie whities? And that change of events (or underwear) could prove very beneficial to both your environments.

"Interesting" is code for "freak" or "boring as hell."

Should someone posing as a friend attempt to set you up with an "interesting" guy, kindly thank them and say, "Oh, geez, I almost forgot. I'm having sharp sticks inserted into my eyes tonight and every night 'til the end of time."

Corollary: "Rent a movie" is code for "let's make out."

When you've gone on a few dates with a guy and he invites you over to his place to "rent a movie," he's really saying, "I'd like to take your body out for a short test drive. Before we go any further, I'd like to see how it feels to sit behind the wheel of your small automobile." Ready to head out on the highway? Then race on over to Blockbuster. Engine idling on low? Not ready for passengers? Cruise on over to the big screen, share some popcorn, and enjoy a ride in the slow lane.

And another Corollary: White lies are not lies.

If they were, they'd simply be called "lies" and they're not. They're called "white lies." Use them liberally (especially when reporting on the outcome of your so-called "interesting" date).

Men should wear engagement rings.

When a guy asks a woman to marry him, she immediately announces to the world she is off the market by sporting a pretty rock (sometimes the size of which would cause her to drown were she accidentally to fall off a bridge). Meanwhile, her male counterpart appears single the entire length of the engagement. What's up with that?

Corollary: Married men should not go ringless in bars.

Contrary to a certain subgroup's popular opinion, instantaneous singlehood is not achieved by removal of the wedding ring. While marauding as a ringless man, you may look and possibly feel single, but guess what? You are not. Go home and put your ring back on.

When a guy you're interested in says, "I'll call you," rely on it as you would your local weather report.

Saying this phrase is akin to hiccuping or kicking when the doctor bangs your knee with a rubber mallet—it's an uncontrollable, reflexive response. Stop thinking the guy will actually call and stop being disappointed when he doesn't.

Corollary: Guys you don't care about will contact you with the precision of a Swiss watch.

And when you don't return their calls, they'll call again and again. Show compassion by nipping these in the bud. A simple, "Thank you, no thank you," message left on voice mail is all that's required—unless you've done the deed and then a voice-to-voice "No, thank you" is, in my book, *de rigeur*.

Double Corollary with a Cherry on Top: Desperation reeks like bad perfume (remember Charley?).

You know you're desperate when you take the actions (or, more likely, the inactions) of strangers personally (i.e. when a guy you barely know says he'll call and doesn't, you immediately go into a mental tailspin, your self-esteem plummets, and you find yourself heading straight to the compost pile for a heaping helping of worm lutefisk). Is it disappointing (the lack of call—not the lutefisk)? Sure. Is it rude? Absolutely. But does it merit self-flagellation and a day of hair-shirt wearing? No way! Repeat after me: A strong internal sense of self is neither dependent on nor swayed by random acts of rude strangers and senseless acts of ugly men.

Show interest 'til disinterested, not vice versa.

There's plenty of time to show disinterest, like how about for the rest of your life. Feigning interest when unsure of your interest level buys time until your brain and heart can confer. Of course, if you stand on one foot and then the other long enough, the other person just might make a decision for you! End of worries.

Corollary: People you do not like like you due to the Concentric Circle Theory.

When someone you don't care for cares for you (or God forbid—vice versa), it's because the care-er has a smaller circle of needs/wants/interests that reside within your larger circle. So while you satisfy all of their needs and interests, they satisfy a mere slice of yours. Phenomenon explained. Move on.

Ambivalence *is* an answer.

Finally, a definitive, mathematically sound, statistically proven response to the age-old syndrome of "ambivalent boyfriend." When a mate tells you he isn't sure he wants to be with you, thank him because, as painful as it may be, you're now sure you don't want to be with him for the following reason:

* What you need to hear: I want to be with you.
* What he says: I'm not sure I want to be with you.

(HINT: I want to be with you ≠ I'm not sure I want to be with you.)

Corollary: Beware the serial monogamist.

Unable to be alone yet afraid of commitment, this guy ends one relationship only to begin another (lather, rinse, repeat). The first time you spend the night, you'll feel right at home with his ready supply of tampons and girl accoutrements accruing quietly at the back of his trusty medicine cabinet. Make your mark before getting adios-ed by adding a few of your own to the pile!

Corollary Shmorollary: Beware the date who phones home.

If you're on a first date and the guy brings his cell phone to dinner, guess what he's bringing to bed? His phone? Worse! Everything that goes with it, including his attitude but minus the part that makes you vibrate.

Never talk about past relationships on a first date.

I am hard-pressed to come up with a good reason why people feel the need to discuss past loves with someone they hardly know, yet may be interested in. Perhaps it's the "I'm not a loser who needs to be dating" syndrome. While it is somewhat comforting to reminisce about a past warm and fuzzy relationship, if you make that mistake often enough with new people, that's all you'll end up doing: reminiscing. Now's the time to jump into the present and lay the groundwork for a newer, warmer, and fuzzier relationship.

Corollary: A new boyfriend is never really new.

Unless you're dating jailbait, your "new" boyfriend is someone else's pre-owned, gently-used model. But were they indeed gently used or are there large Samsonites just waiting to be unpacked? Peek behind door No. 1 and find out!

Size (and girth) matters!

Whoever said size doesn't matter must have been a pin dick or be married to one. Come on, right?!

Sort of a Corollary: More thoughts on size.

It is a travesty that a woman's "size" (see: breast) is advertised for all the world to see, while men are afforded the luxury of hiding their eighth wonder of the world until you've been charmed by their:

* witty banter
* large wallets
* five martinis

Run from a boyfriend who hates his mother.

If a guy detests his mother, run for the nearest set of hills. "Run," I say, "run!" In a case like this, you can't lace up your sneakers fast enough, for the simple fact that a mother is a son's role model for women and "detests his mother" translates into funky, ambivalent feelings for the entire female gender (see: Ambivalence is an answer). If you're in the market for a guy to funk with your head, then this is the man for you!

Corollary: A boyfriend must love your dog or do a great job of faking it.

When a potential boyfriend doesn't like your dog, I have an easy-to-follow rule of thumb. It's called: Next! All you dog owners out there, I think you know where I'm coming from. And if he doesn't like your cat, well, he just might be a keeper....

Weekend dates are more meaningful than weekday dates.

The importance of acknowledging this truth is to make sense of the subtle, unspoken language of dating. Say you have progressed to the second or third date and your partner does not ask for a weekend date. You are not meriting weekend-date status. So, even if your date can't actually verbalize, "I'm not terribly interested," he is indeed saying it. Read the writing on the wall.

Corollary: Saturday night dates are even more important than Friday night dates.

They just are. Read it and weep.

Important relationships take so long to get over due to Euphoric Recall.

There is a mental gyration women go through when they end with a significant other. It's progressive and goes something like this:

1. Ohhh, I miss him so much!
2. The way he used to...and how we were going to...
3. Well, actually, he never really did...
4. What a...!
5. Boy, am I glad he's out of my life!

Problem is, women often fall off this thought process mid-gyration, right around No. 2. They get stuck recalling only the good memories, go into a mini-mental tailspin, and wind up calling their girlfriends if they're lucky or their exes if they're not.

Corollary: Ex-lovers are not meant to be friends.

Men and women who routinely transform past lovers into friends are either (A) half Borg, or (B) were never very much in love to begin with. Does it happen occasionally? Sure, see (B). Is it part of the natural order of things? No, see (A).

Love happens when you least expect it.

Translated, this reads: think of the thing you most want in the world. Got it? Now pretend you don't want it! Along the lines of clearing-your-mind-while-meditating, I classify this concept as one of those unresolvable Zen riddles specifically designed to drive single people insane.

Corollary: There is no such thing as meaningless sex.

Most women I know prefer to have sex within the context of a loving relationship, but when Mr. Right is indisposed, many often find themselves singing the praises of Mr. Right Now. Therefore, meaningless sex—that is sex of the "wham, bam, (give or take a) thank you, ma'am" genre—while scratching the itch, also serves to remind us of what's missing. Meaningless sex highlights the plethora of meaninglessness—sexual or otherwise—in one's life. Meaningless sex can, in a weird way, be a wake-up call. By alerting oneself to the void, there's a good chance of changing it. Someday. Does everyone need a good bang once in a while? Sure, which is why there's such a thing as meaningless sex.

Corollary to the Corollary: Last-time sex is like looking at an oncoming train in a rear-view mirror—you can only define it in retrospect.

When in a relationship that's heading south, neither party wants to acknowledge their final passionate hour (or minute) in bed. So, while you may have an inkling of impending doom, it is unlikely if interviewed at the moment of consummation you could definitively say, "Yes, this is the last time I will be hiding this man's salami."

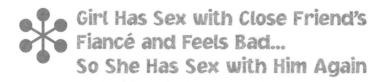
Dear Laurie,

About five weeks ago, I had sex with a close friend's boyfriend while I was drunk. A week later, he proposed to her. I don't like him and feel really guilty. Then I slept with him again two weeks after they were engaged. Afterward, he wanted me to say that I loved him, but I wouldn't because I don't. I told him how wrong I felt for being with him and he said that it was his fault, not mine. Now every time I see him he acts like he likes me and he always wants to look into my eyes. It's starting to really get to me. His fiancée thinks I'm just the greatest person ever because she doesn't know a thing. She is also very obsessed with him. What should I do now?

Awful, slutty friend

Dear "Awful, Slutty Friend,"

Let me get this straight. You slept with your friend's fiancé and felt bad about it, so to undo the bad ju-ju you set in motion, you applied the use of the double-negative and slept with him again. Ohhhh. I don't get it.

I have to agree. As far as friends go, you are an awful one. I'm not sure if I would necessarily call you slutty, if that makes you feel any better (I'd need to know how many other friends' boyfriends you were bagging). I also don't know what you were doing sleeping with a guy you supposedly don't like. Oh, yeah, you were drunk. Shall I assume you were drunk the second time you slept with him, too? Are you always drunk? Or are you too afraid to admit that, in a very weird way, you like being part of this love triangle? Thoughts for food...

So what's the question here? Let me reread. Oh, right, what you should do:

1. Stop screwing your friend's fiancé.
2. In order to accomplish No. 1, I further suggest you stop partying with/hanging around your friend's fiancé. If you can't control yourselves in each other's company, then get out of each other's company. It's that simple.
3. Not that you asked me, but *do not* tell your supposed girl-friend about what's gone/going on. I'm sure on some unconscious level she has a clue that all is not right in the house of love, but the obsessed heart has a miraculous way of cajoling the sensible head to go on holiday. Hers is far off on the world's most remote island, Tristan da Cunha. It is not your job to rip her out of fantasyland—you have done quite enough already. This multitasking, narcissistic buffoon you keep boinking will blow the whole thing sky high all by himself—on that you can rely.
4. See No.1.

I have to go back to a point touched on earlier in paragraph one. While you know you are behaving inappropriately, you continue to do so. What a conundrum. Is the devil making you do it? People do things—inappropriately or otherwise—because it benefits them. I won't even begin to conjecture about monsieur fiancé's motivation, but I would like to touch briefly on what you're getting out of this. Let's see: you don't have a boyfriend and your "close friend" does. Hmm. Perhaps we're feeling a little attention deprived and maybe just a tad, wee bit, jealous of our good friend who's getting married. Perhaps? Yes?

Perhaps. Those are very basic human emotions to have, but it's not very nice to act on those feelings in the way you have *chosen* to do. Yes, while it may be easier to pretend you've fallen—without will—headlong into this whirling vortex of deceit and indiscretion, truth be told, you *decided* to do it. Woe is *toi*.

The short answer: Are you a horrible person? No. Does your behavior leave something to be desired? Yes. Start behaving. Stop wasting your time booty-callin' your friend's booty and go out and find some of your own. And then when you do, maybe your good friend will write in about how bad she feels having sex with *your* fiancé....

Lovingly&logically yours,
Laurie

Girl Blows Friends (Off) for Guy

Dear Laurie,

I've been going out with this guy for a while now. The thing is, we go to different schools so we don't see each other often. Now that school's out, we've been hanging out pretty much every night and all my girls from my school are getting upset at me. They are feeling left out now that I don't spend much time with them anymore. And now I don't know what to do to keep them both happy. I mean, I want to be with my boyfriend all the time, but I just never have time for any of my school friends anymore. What should I do to keep them both happy? Anything would help. Thanks.

Lisa

Dear Lisa,

Learn this lesson and learn it quick: a girl does *not* drop her friends for a guy. Don't get me wrong—gals do it *all the time* (ohmygod do they do it), but they should *not*. It is so lame on so many levels. Let me shed some light for you.

Reason No. 1

When you have relationship trauma (which you will, *trust* me on this one), who you going to call? And don't think after completely shining on Denise, Starla, Bashon, or whatever the hell your friends' names are, they are going to take your call. Uh uh, girlfriend, because at that point you would be what we call a "fair-weather friend." Git it? Available when it suits you and unavailable when it don't. Who needs that?

Reason No. 2

When you get dumped, who you going to hang with when you're feeling (and looking) like a jumbo pile o' poo? When every other word out of your mouth is from broken-record hell? Cross Stevie, DeRon, Brit, and Carrie off your list, sweetheart, because they are *in*-disposed! Best sidle up to your favorite Backstreet 'N Sync-y Boys CD and ride out that storm so-lo!

Reason No. 3

How's about when you decide José is no longer floating your gravy train and you need to *adios* his sorry ass? Then what are you going to do with *all* the time you were spending with boyfriend-boy? Got any spring cleaning to do?

Reason No. 4

Imagine you're single again (hard to fathom, I know, but shit happens), and Sheila, who is your absolute-fave, hang-out-at-the-rave, who's-last-penny-you-once-gave girlfriend, starts seeing Bryan "pretty much every night" and "all her girls" (including yourself) "from her school are getting upset" at her "and are feeling left out now that" Sheila doesn't "spend much time with them" (and you) "anymore." Have you grabbed my point as it whizzed by your boyfriend-dazed head? Some day the shoe will be on the other Candies-totin' foot, sweetheart, and how's that going to feel? In fact, sometime far off in the future, you may *finally* understand what your friends are feeling right now. Won't that be quite the en-lightening bolt?!

Reason No. 5

The last reason why a girl shouldn't dump her friends for a guy: because if you are lucky enough to have a true friend (whether you're single or not), someone who you click with, can relate to, and be 96 percent honest with, well, honey, that is a rare find and you need to hold on to her! Let her know how much you appreciate her. Nourish a find like that and every time it blooms, it will amaze you.

Oh, and believe it or not, even if you and what's-his-face stay together, at some point, the two of you will feel less smitten and will feel the need to resume your regularly scheduled lives. At that point, you'll do the friendship yodel only to hear its empty echo come right back atcha!

The short answer: Everything in moderation. Lisa, you've got a guy you're jazzed about. *Great*! I understand you only get to see him for the summer, but you do not need to see him "every night"—that's excessive. Here's how I see the scenario: two measly nights a week you don't see Joe Blow. Instead, you see your friends. That leaves *five* nights to see Joe—plenty! Can you handle that? And if not seeing him makes you feel like an insulin-dependent diabetic without insulin, then like all diabetics, you may want to get yourself to a doctor.

Lovingly&logically yours,
Laurie

Teen Virgin Queries:
Should I Stay (a Virgin) or
Should I Go (Have Sex) Now?

Dear Laurie,

I'm sixteen and I'm still a virgin. I want to have sex, but all these questions run through my head. How will it be? Will I catch something? Will I get pregnant? Will it hurt? So should I just wait or should I just go ahead and do it?

Anxious

Dear "Anxious,"

You're sixteen and probably have been wearing a bra for only two years—maybe three if you're lucky. Do you even have your license (to drive, not wear a bra)? I think girls should have puberty firmly under their belts before they take the sex plunge, which would put you around eighteen or nineteen before you partake of the all-you-can-eat sausage-fest buffet for $9.99.

This is all a not-so-thinly veiled attempt to come right out and say, "Sixteen is way too freakin' young to be having god-damn sex, young lady!" especially if you're so unsure/scared of it (which you are and should be at your age, by the way). Having said that, I am happy to answer all of your questions.

Question 1: "How will it be?"

It'll suck. You'll be scared. You may get your cherry broken (that's *hymen* for you techies out there), which means you'll bleed all over your nice clean sheets (or the back seat of a random car). You certainly won't have an orgasm, unless you're related to the Amazon Sex Clan of Women from the Moon. When it's over, you'll silently ask yourself, "Is that it?" and wonder why you skipped going to the movies with your friends.

First-time sex is all about getting through the experience so you can tell your uninitiated girlfriends that you "did it." The eager looks on said friends' faces will quickly have you lying through your teeth about the whole god-awful experience. Some girlfriends you'll tell will have already done it and the two of you will smile knowingly at each other—knowing that it sucked for both of you and that you're both pretending it didn't. Sex doesn't get good (I'm talking really good) until you're in your thirties, so buckle up and sit tight for safety, sister!

When I lost my virginity, I called my then best college friend, Carol, from California the morning after (please note the use of the word *college* in conjunction with the losing of the virginity). She had already lost hers the summer before to Horatio while leaning against a fence, so I felt like I had some catching up to do (which is a silly reason to "do it," but pretty much why we all do it in the first place anyway). I think circus calliope music would best sum up the evening's events for me—a veritable blur of clothing articles flying and body parts flashing by.

From the sound of your note, it seems like you might be missing one crucial element: a partner with whom you will toss your burdensome virginity. Don't forget, to have intercourse, a partner is key. A loving partner is even better. But, for the first time, let's not get too carried away. If you don't currently have a boyfriend, that isn't to say you won't be able to find an infinite number of boys who would willingly oblige an eager virgin like yourself. Last time I checked the section "Boys Willing to Deflower Virgins," the listings had to be archived on CD-ROM.

Question 2: "Will I catch something?"

If you are "fast" enough, you can catch all sorts of things. Use a condom, girl! You know, those plastic packages that burn a hole in every teenage guy's back pocket. The ones they gave you bananas to practice with in sex ed class. Maybe that was just my sex ed—or my fantasy of it. Oh, and don't go sleeping with every Tom, Dick, or Harry (especially Dick) because then your bingo odds go way up.

Question 3: "Will I get pregnant?"

This question scares me, as it doesn't seem "we" (royal) quite get how the whole process works. If you don't use any birth control (condom!), there's a great chance you'll get pregnant. Do you have parents? Can you talk to them? Stupid question? How about a school counselor or teacher you like? I know, more stupid questions. At least you're talking to me (which you'd think would be enough incentive to get all those other people talking to you instead).

In a nutshell, you can get pregnant any time during your period cycle, but you are most fertile smack dab in the middle of it. Have you had your period yet? Have you read, *Are You There God? It's Me, Margaret* or *Deenie* or *Forever?* If you've answered "no" to any of the last four questions, then you for sure aren't ready for sex. Back in the 70s, no self-respecting girl would've even considered heavy petting—let alone having sex—without first consulting Judy Blume! Kids these days....

Question 4: "Will it hurt?"

Not if you're really drunk. Oh, but I digress. Yes, it will hurt some. See question No.1: "How will it be?"

Question 5: "So should I just wait or should I just go ahead and do it?"

Wait! Wait. I think you should wait. Do you get the feeling I think you might want to shelve this idea for a while? In the name of you-don't-know-what-the-hell-you're-thinking-or-feeling about all this, again, I say, "Whoa, sister!"

The short answer: Sex is physically intimate. You take all your clothes off and roll around together, which can be really cool if you're with the right person and an absolute disaster if you're not. It's important that your first experience be a positive one! Not being ready—feeling anxious—is a surefire way to capsize your maiden voyage. Think about it some more. Try talking it over with a close friend or two. Find yourself a good guy. When you're really ready, you won't have to ask anyone but yourself. Don't give in to peer pressure—it's so 8os....

Lovingly&logically yours,
Laurie

Dear Laurie,

I did something kind of bitchy and my boyfriend then actually called me a "bitch" (!), which, regardless of my behavior, was very hurtful and, I think, way out of line. Since then, he's apologized and tried to take back what he said, but I can't seem to forgive and forget. What should I do?

Hurt in Houston

Good morning, class! Today's lesson is on responsibility. Can you say R-E-S-P-O-N-S-I-whatever...? Okay, Miss Hurt, you yourself admit you were acting bitchy and your man friend then called you on it. The old adage, "words will never hurt me" (which, by the way, was probably written by a deaf mute), is B.S. as you have experienced. But if you're going to act a certain way, i.e. bitchy, then step up to the plate and take responsibility for it. For every action, there is an equal and opposite reaction, i.e. what goes up must come down and its corollary—what gets bitchy must get yelled at.

So, lesson No. 248 is: If you choose to do something (and life is all about choice), then be prepared to take the consequences (good or bad). Suggestion No. 359 is: Try to understand your underlying needs and wants and express them directly, instead of acting in a certain way, i.e. bitchy, in the hopes your mate will read your mind and figure out what the hell you really want!

The short answer: Accept your boyfriend's heartfelt apology (you were lucky to get it) and stop acting like a bitch.

Lovingly&logically yours,
Laurie

Baggage

He loves me and my baggage...

He loves me and my baggage NOT...

He loves me AND my baggage...

four

The Five Stages of Being Single (Again):

Be a "Been There, Done That" Master

Whether you were the dumper or dumpee makes little difference when readjusting to Lifestyles of the Moderately Well-Paid and Single. Lucky for all of us, psychologists have painstakingly researched the healing process. Will this information help speed recovery? No, but isn't it reassuring to point out where you are on the continuum while lying curled up and sniveling on the floor?

Because being single is not addictive, this process occurs in stages, not steps, and there are only five of them (you get seven off for relatively good behavior, I suppose).

Stage 1: Denial

Denial is nice and straightforward. It's a near-Herculean mental commitment to the prior status quo. It goes something like this: "I still have a boyfriend. I just won't be seeing him... ever again."

Stage 2: Anger

The anger stage is full of foot stomping and whiney wails of "Why me?!" and "Why not my bitch neighbor?!"

Stage 3: Bargaining

Bargaining often takes place before the loss, so why it's number three is a mystery to me. Unless you're psychic or a compulsive planner, skip this stage and go directly to depression (Stage 4).

Deal-making is indicative of the bargaining stage. "Buying a condo" or "announcing an IPO" are not examples of bargaining stage deal-making. Similar to Lent or avoiding yeast products during Passover, bargaining-type deals require sacrifice, i.e. swearing off manicures or six months of massages, in return for whomever you have lost.

Stage 4: Depression

Scouting out tall bridges and clocking fast-moving buses are favorite pastimes of anger and bargaining graduates. Do try and refrain from performing irreversible acts of depression, since acceptance of your lousy state of affairs is right around the corner!

Stage 5: Acceptance

Acceptance is the final stage of being single again. And it's a hard one! You have to be content with what you don't want: your singlehood! And no faking it, either (that's for later—when you're no longer single).

Acceptance requires washing off the putridly sweet Eau de Desperation you've been dousing yourself in and replacing it with the intoxicating yet sophisticated scent of contentment. Men come running out of the woodwork at near-illegal speeds when they catch the tiniest whiff of true contentment (Eau de Desperation causes an equal yet opposite effect).

Acceptance is one of those enlightenment things. If that's too heavy for you, buy one of those mini babbling brooks (complete with rocks and motor) for $49.95 and call it a day.

Teach a Girl

GIVE
a girl a date
and she'll
eat one nice
dinner...

TEACH
a girl to date
and she'll
have her
whole house
redecorated!

Sex-Crazed Woman Wantonly Uses the "L" Word

NOTE: Comments in capital letters and parentheses are mine.

Dear Laurie,

Okay...I have heard this rule before. (SHE'S HEARD THE RULE!) *Don't tell the guy you love him first. Well, I broke that rule.* (SHE BROKE THE RULE!) *I told my boyfriend I loved him because I do, and felt like I could not not* (SHE USED A DOUBLE NEGATIVE!) *let him know how I truly feel about him. He did not reply to me telling him I loved him....* (HE DID NOT REPLY!) *He is the most wonderful person I have ever met and I feel closer to him as a friend than the people who are already friends in my life.* (SHE IS IN A SEX HAZE!) *He is recently divorced, our relationship has moved very quickly, and it scares him a little. Yet he likes the relationship* (I.E. THE SEX) *and doesn't want to change the way things are going. I am so confused! I care about him more than anything* (I.E., SHE LIKES THE SEX, TOO!), *but should I let things slow down? Keep things the way they are? Move to a different city and go under the witness protection program* (NOW SHE'S TALKING!)? *Did I mention he sent me two dozen long stem roses the day after our first date (SHE DIDN'T MENTION IT!)? I feel very fortunate to have him in my life and need to know what the next step is...sigh.*

Dear "Sigh,"

I am no medical doctor, but if I had to venture a diagnosis, I would say you, my dear, are experiencing the classic side effects of a Scooty High. This is a condition that results from having received a higher than normal dose of HBI (more commonly known as the Hot Beef Injection). Commonly disorienting, though never lethal, Scooty High symptoms include:

* jumping in quickly
* thinking someone is the most wonderful person you have ever met
* confusion!
* saying, "I love you" first

Man, Sigh, you could not be more textbook! Chill out! Ca-hooool it. What is your hurry? I know I sound like an absolute boor, but you are currently not of this Earth. And don't get me wrong, new relationships and especially new sex can be Fa-han-tast-tique, but the mojo-induced adrenaline and state of yippy-kay-yay euphoria you are experiencing is not real. Remember, you've got an abnormal amount of serotonin or whatever the brain chemical is that allows rats when lab-tested to ignore the food button and push the chemically induced orgasm button to the point where they starve themselves and die.

Listen to yourself:

1. You think your new boyfriend is more of a friend to you than your current stable o' friends. No, he's not. True friendship must stand the test of time and foul weather. It doesn't sound like you two have had time for either. Boy, will you be grateful for those proud few who are still around after you float down from your cloud.

2. You "care about him more than anything." Uh, I'm gonna puke.

3. You said the "L" word first. Clearly a sign that you are not of sound mind. And he didn't say it back—that's his deer-in-the-headlights way of saying, "Whoa, Nellie!" And the dozen roses thing *apres le* first date? Big deal. Stakes are low at that point. He can pour it on. It's a nice, albeit somewhat over-the-top, gesture, but I wouldn't read too much into it.

Your dude is "recently divorced" and your "relationship has moved very quickly, and it scares him a little." The first sign of sanity—hallelujah! It should scare you, too, honey. Let me explain what "recently divorced" means. "Recently divorced" means your guy is from the land of black and white. His ex is black (bad, boring, a nag, now nothing more than a whiny dollar sign) and you are white (pure, temporarily perfect, Miss Twenty-Four-Rose, do-no-wrong). But guess what? You, too, someday will be black in his eyes, as he will be in yours—it's human nature. People we love get on our nerves. The question is, when that happens, will he stick around? Will you guys be able to continue feeling the love?

The short answer: I don't mean to sound like the biggest grinch on the face of this lovin' Earth, but get a grip. Snap to. Strike a pose—I mean a balance. Step back and ask yourself if this guy has the qualities you're looking for in a long-term mate. Does he treat you well over time? And if there are more yeses to these questions than nos, then proceed with caution. You have nothing but time—your newly divorced boyfriend is not jumping into marriage again anytime soon, on that you can depend! In the meantime, attend to your friendships! Reacquaint yourself with their worth because, in the end, they are what nurture and support us through these wild rides. Yeah, you betcha!

Lovingly&logically yours,
Laurie

He Loves Me (not),
He Loves Me not,
He Loves Me (not)...

Hi Laurie,

Good to have someone to talk to about my problem. I am a thirty-year-old woman with a boy who's eight, divorced (three years), and madly and passionately in love with a fairly handsome photographer who happens to be my neighbor.

He's single, we are together for a little more than a year now, but the problem is he is still not sure if he loves me or not. He wants to get married and live with someone for the rest of his life, maybe even have kids, but he is not convinced I am that someone.

He's so very honest about everything—he always tells me when he is doubtful about our relationship. He says there are times he knows almost for sure that we will get married in the end, but there are also many times he's not so sure at all. He's been alone for more than ten years. I do hope you'll write me an answer because I would very much like to know how you would deal with a case like this.

Yours truly, Zoë

Dear Zoë,

A year is plenty of time for two mature adults to know if they are in love with each other (I'll bet anything this guy is in his early forties and not just because I'm good at math). Those who say they don't know typically are either incapable of love or do know and are afraid to say it.

Zoë, dear—do you have a pair of running shoes? Because you need to put them on right now. Lace them up nice and tight and run for the nearest set of hills. And just before you take off, don't forget to lace up a pair of shoes for your son, too. He deserves a better male role model than this noncommittal drip (by seeking one, you'll be a better female model, too).

This guy, who's been alone for more than ten years (oh, what a surprise), ain't going to come around. For whatever reason, he's missing the relate-ability gene or it fell out of his pocket along the way or it was revoked at some point. And he's mean—giving you an emotional weather report every hour on the hour. Who asked? You say he's "honest," I prefer to call him neurotic, but you're a better euphemist than I.

In addition to a pair of running shoes, Zoë, do you have a fishing pole? Get one and swallow it in the hope that your sense of self and self-esteem may bite and you can haul them up from the depths of your soul. The only kind of woman who waits around with this kind of guy is one who doesn't feel she's worthy of much more and I suspect that might be you.

The short answer: Tell Mr. Passive-Aggressive Manipulator-Shit-Heel that all relationships are fraught with I-love-you/ I-don't-love-you (why do you think Matt Groening's cartoon,

Life in Hell, is so popular?!). The difference between this guy and the rest of the world is that mature, compassionate people do not have to broadcast every feeling and can deal with the anxiety that life's twists and turns provoke. That or they have a very good shrink.

Lovingly&logically yours,
Laurie

Saved from the Future Ex
Josh, 42
How We Met: Outside of SpeedDating

For the uninitiated, SpeedDating is (according to the market-ing-ese on the website) "an exciting, quick, and nonpressured way to meet quality singles. In one evening, you'll meet seven people in individual, one-on-one conversations of seven minutes each."

The bell rings (literally) and you start chatting. No talking about what you do for a living or directly asking the person out (that's the nonpressured part). The bell rings again and you're done—buh-bye! Then you fill out your score card. You write the name and number of your SpeedDate on the line provided, and check the appropriate box: "Yes, I'd like to see this person again" or "No, seven minutes was more than enough, thank you." If both people say "yes," the guy is given the woman's number and asked to call within three days. One "yes" and one "no" equals no go.

When I first walked in to register, a three-hundred-pound Jerry Garcia look-alike was writing out a check. Suavely, I bypassed the sign-in desk, ran to the bathroom, and called a friend. After a short chat, I reasoned with myself: I hadn't showered, put on makeup, worn contact lenses, dressed up, and valet parked for nothing! Besides it was the holiday season—Christmas was right around the corner, so I decided to experiment with some holiday cheer. I ordered a 7&7 and took out my checkbook (Rule No. 1: Do not drink while SpeedDating! It impairs your dating vision.

Makes you say "yes" when you should say "no." Gives you an overly elevated sense of compassion for those speeding around you).

I first saw Josh standing at the bar, but when the "dating" began, he was nowhere to be seen. I later learned he'd come early to survey the crowd, found it not to his liking, and skipped out...to attend a Klezmer concert. Naturally.

Josh was handsome—not a hottie, but pleasing to look at. Ironically, as I said, we met outside of SpeedDating afterward on the street corner. I was waiting for a friend. At the same time, Josh was on his way back from the Klezmer concert to meet up with a friend who had actually stayed and SpeedDated. As Josh crossed the street and came closer, I remembered seeing him in the bar. And, clearly, he remembered seeing me.

Josh: *So, how was SpeedDating?*

Me: *What? Is it written across my forehead? (Pause.) You were in there, weren' t you? And you left!*

Remember earlier I said Josh "surveyed the crowd, found it not to his liking..."? Hey, wait a minute, I was part of that crowd and he recognized me...could somebody please do the math on that one?

We chatted briefly, exchanging business cards within three minutes thereby breaking all recorded land-speed records for dating (seven? please!). Was it the residual effects of the 7&7? His handsome, not-hottie face? My desperation at having just "dated" seven Jerry Garcias? Who can truly say?

To make a short story medium-length, Josh verified my hunch that attractive, forty-two-year-old men are unmarried for a reason. (The reason varies, but if you look closely at the tag on the inside, it's there.) After several lengthy email and phone exchanges, the only night we could agree to get together was December 24, Christmas Eve.

I need to clue you all in on a Jewish Christmas ritual. It's called The Matzoh Ball. It's a singles party—a place where people with no good dating prospects go. Josh had his forty-two-year-old heart set on going. Again: what is the Matzoh Ball? It's a place where people with no good dating prospects go. Oh. Hmm.

Josh then asked if it would be possible for me to dine with him early, around 5:30 PM—thereby maximizing his Matzoh time. On behalf of myself and women penciled in the world over I said, "Sounds great, let me get back to you on that," and speedily lost his number.

five

Finding Mr. Produce:

*Love's Potential among
the Fruits and Vegetables*

I often wonder where my (future) husband is while I'm out and about doing my "thang." What's he doing? Who's he hanging with? Does he miss me? In honor of this whacked-out thought process, I present this little ditty:

> In the produce aisle,
> (I was too lazy to go to last night),
> I imagine stood Mr. Right:
> Smelling pears and pressing peaches.
>
> Did he know
> I was supposed to go,
> And wait?
>
> Or did he instead
> Cock his head
> And smile at the blond weighing cabbage?

When Stephen picks me up looking exactly as he did at the party at which I met him, I am disappointed. (I was hoping somehow he would show up transformed.)

I accept his current appearance and look forward to my upcoming, post-vodka tonic review. As we leave my apartment and walk down the street, I'm wondering which is his car, all the while hoping it isn't the '76 white Pontiac LeMans we get into.

We go to Chinatown and eat—Chinese food fried every which way to Sunday. I could swear we have the same dish seven times, but I am quite hungry and so, relatively, it is okay. Conversation is better than everything previously described, which isn't saying a whole lot. Stephen is bright, no doubt about that, but at thirty-seven he still isn't particularly inter-ested in marriage (-8 points) or very interested in wearing decent clothes (-2).

With dinner over (he pays: +2), we stroll back to 1976. On the way, he can tell I am chilly so he very chivalrously offers me his jacket (+10). I am touched and put it on thinking, I wish I were digging this guy's chili. As we stroll down the street, I put my hands in the coat pockets (it's a Dennis-the-Menace-type jacket: thin, blue, waist high, zip-up—these details mean noth-ing to the story...).

As we approach the car, he puts his hand out for the keys which are in the pocket of the coat I am wearing. I pull out the keys, a packet of gum, some Kleenex, and something else comes out, too. It falls onto the cement sidewalk. Reflexively, we both look down. Intuitively, I know what it is and as I'm bending down to pick it up I'm wondering what I'll do with it once I get it: "it" being a brand new, shiny condom (-20), "Black Stealth" (-10) (not "stealth" at all, really).

My first, nice-Laurie inclination is to casually kick it into the gutter, but then I think, how often do you get the chance to exploit a situation like this? So, I pick it up and say, "Whaaaat's that?!" Whether it was for me or some other lucky gal, I couldn't tell you. His attempt at recovery was to suggest we go "make out." So we did...NOT!

Total score: -28 (That'd be no score.)

Male Order

Should Seventeen-Year-Old Girl Date Twenty-Eight-Year-Old Pervert?

Dear Laurie,
I'm turning 18 next year and this twenty-eight-year-old guy, who only looks nineteen, likes me and I like him, but I'm not sure I should go out with him.

Dear Jailbait:

Let me get this straight: you're seventeen (turning eighteen *next* year—seventeen one year, eighteen the next...funny how that works), looking to date a twenty-eight-year old?!?!?!?!? No way, I say. No, wait, did I say "no way"? Oh good, 'cause I meant, "no way." God help me...and you...and *him*...God help each and every one of us!

So he looks nineteen: that's like telling me he's right-handed. I don't care what he looks like. Do I type like I care what he looks like? What was it I didn't say that made you think I cared about what he looks like? Let me be perfectly clear: looks shmooks.

I once dated a guy who didn't look his age, which basically translated directly into he didn't act his age (B-A-D, bad). Internalizing society's younger perception of yourself can stunt some people's emotional growth. They don't look grown up, therefore aren't expected to act grown up, and so they don't grow up. Society has certain expectations of people at certain ages. Granted, we do not want to run our lives by others' perceptions, but nor do we want to live completely outside the range of acceptibility (hint: Mr. Jailbaiter is outside normal ranges. Statistically speaking, we would call him an outlier. Guys like these throw the bell curve *way off*.).

At certain ages, we do certain things to further our growth as individuals, i.e. between the ages of about twenty-seven to forty-two, men look for appropriate partners to marry (not go to Britney Spears concerts with). Fact o' the matter is, boyfriend is twenty-eight. That's one-score-and-eight as opposed to your one-score-minus-three—in other words, no score. Does that help clarify the matter? Thought so. This guy's almost thirty and the best he can do is cradle-rob a seventeen-year-old???? Spooky. Creepy. Cruddy. Gross. Excuse me while I puke and brush my teeth....

I'm back. Seems to me, I've heard this story before, like as the lead headline for the six o'clock news: "Twenty-eight-year-old pervert-weirdo molests and leaves for dead seventeen-year-old naïve-hopeful looking for true love in all the wrong places." Don't you wonder what a supposedly grown man wants with a slightly post-pubescent teenage girl? I mean, duh, we know what he wants, but why can't he go pick on someone his own age? Because he's too emotionally ill-equipped to appeal to a grown woman his own age. *That's* why!

I know that with impressionable youths like yourself I'm not supposed to emphatically tell you what you should and should not do because then, the math follows, you'll do exactly what I say you should not do and you won't do exactly what I say you should. But guess what?! I'm giving you a little more credit than that. I'm assuming you have a brain inside that hormonally raging, slightly befuddled head of yours (double reverse psychology with a back flip, degree of difficulty: 5.6). I'm going to figure you'll take what I say with a small grain of Kosher rock salt and make an intelligent, well-thought-out decision for yourself based on all the gripping arguments I have set forth. And if you don't, well then, I'll keep a lookout for you on channel seven.

The short answer: Go find yourself a nice eighteen, nineteen, or twenty-year-old. Preferably someone with whom you have shared interests beyond playing hide the salami (not a bad game, but it's nice to have stuff to talk about afterward). In the meantime, stop hanging around, emailing, phoning, psychically conjuring this twenty-eight-year-old perv. Let him be someone else's therapy problem—I guarantee, in a few years' time, you'll thank me heartily.

Lovingly&logically yours,
Laurie

Getting Down

six

Over My Dead Body or Aided-Dating Methods 101:

A Worldwide Web of Men Awaits!

Just as a job seeker taps many resources to find the job of his/her dreams so, too, should a mate seeker add aided methods, i.e. Internet dating, to the arsenal of weapons in the fight against singlehood.

The matchmaking concept has been around since time immemorial and since time immemorial, people have complained about it. The fact that we've replaced the whiskered yenta with a keyboard and a mouse is merely a sign of the times. Meeting someone over the Internet does not qualify you as a complete loser. Being a loser qualifies you as a loser! If you aren't a loser prior to placing an ad or a profile, you're not a loser afterward.

There is no shame in dating on the Internet. Okay, there is shame, but these days, what are your alternatives?

Alternative #1: The Bar Scene

And wear yet another unapologetically spilled Cosmopolitan on your back? No, thank you. Do women occasionally meet The

One at a bar? Oh, sure, and these princes are either missing front teeth or merely serve as the exception to the rule.

Alternative #2: Work
Finding true love at the workplace is di-cey! You have one of three options:
- drunken Christmas party screw and its embarrassing aftermath
- one-on-one dating where you dump, get dumped, or marry someone you then have to see 24/7 for the rest of your life
- lawsuit (yours or his)

Alternative #3: The Setup, a.k.a. The Blind Date
Is he a dream or a dud? Usually a dud, but if you are lucky enough to have a friend (a true friend because "friends don't let friends date duds") offer to set you up and then actually do it, one of two things will happen: *The Guinness Book of World Records* will call you up, or you will be married and not reading this book.

Alternative #4: The Grocery Store
Imagine buying food and getting someone to prepare it all in the same place?! Nirvana, eh? But not so fast. Flirting while making buying decisions is always a risky bet. It requires high-level, multitasking ability. Those less skilled often return home with a year's supply of Ramen. Flirter beware.

Alternative #5: The Gym

The gym is an ideal scope center: people aren't drunk, you get a very representative look at the goods, and you share a common, if somewhat lame, interest. Nonetheless, I believe 1988 was the last year in which a man asked a woman out at the gym. She reportedly said, "Sure."

Many people seem to think dating on the Internet is going to be so much different or better or more fun than dating in general. It isn't. Remember those loser singles parties you used to go to? Well, they've all been consolidated, virtually, on the Internet. Now you no longer have to shower or shave to join the party—just sit on your crack and click. That said, Internet dating makes you feel:

* in pseudo control of your dating life
* like there are guys out there to date
* slightly less hopeless about the state of the nonunion

The difference with suitors on the Internet and real-life people is that potential dates on the Internet present better than in real life. They choose a particularly good (read: old) photo or write unusually glowing things (read: lie) about themselves. *Caveat emptor* (translated, that means: run to your nearest cave and hide!). These two-dimensional knights in shining gigabytes rarely translate directly upon a three-dimensional meeting. In other words, take these cyber dudes with an Everest-sized grain of salt. And remember, the delete button is your friend.

Weeding through the myriad of men on Internet sites can take a year's worth of time off your life, so I have a few guiding rules of thumb.

❋ Have picture will chat (and the corollary: no pic-y, no chatty). I'm not a vain, all-about-the-looks bitch, but physical appearance does matter—it's that chemistry thing. Save yourself and cyber-date No. 268 some time and angst by exchanging photos (if not posted) prior to meeting.

❋ Know your threshold basics, i.e. level of education, upper and lower desired age ranges, and marriage status as well as your absolute deal breakers (mine include white supremacists and God-fearing radicals—is that redundant?).

❋ And the safety stuff. Meet in a cool, dry place (that's for Parmesan cheese, never mind). Meet in a public place, let a friend know where you're going, and don't give out contact info prematurely (don't do anything prematurely, for that matter...).

❋ Promote good dating karma by replying to each and every one of your cybersuitors. That's right. If someone went to the trouble of showing interest, you owe him a reply—however modest. A favorite of mine goes something like this: "Thanks for your note, but after reading your profile it seems we don't have enough in common to go forward. Take care, your-fake-online-name here." This response is courteous, promotes goodwill, and covers all rejection reasons under the sun—from rat's ass photo to unrealized scholastic potential. It's a winner. Use it with abandon.

Now that I have you running scared from a round of aided dating, let me toss out a few benefits.

Benefit No. 1

Internet dating keeps you from appearing desperate. You post an interesting profile, you upload a snappy photo, and, before you know it, eight new suitors appear in your mailbox. Are 6.75 of them guys you would never want to talk to in your life? Maybe, but initially they send complimentary letters. Complimentary letters are flattering and flattery makes you feel good. A compliment is always a nice thing, so enjoy it for what it is, be gracious about it, write a nice rejection note, and walk a little taller in the world knowing you're a babe.

Benefit No. 2

Sometimes you meet a cool friend. Perhaps someone invites you to the transmogrified animation festival or shares your interest in xenogenic transplantation. Maybe they lecture on quantum foam and worm holes or...well, the list goes on. Meeting a platonic, kindred spirit is most definitely a good thing.

Benefit No. 3

Look like you're trying to find a mate and get rude yet well-meaning nags (like my sister and perhaps your father) temporarily off your back by joining an aided-dating site. Stop relatives from clipping and sending you the latest "hot" singles' websites from such hip publications as *Time* magazine and *The Wall Street Journal* by simply signing up for a FREE trial membership.

Benefit No. 4

If you're a writer, aided dating gives you fodder to...fodder about. Or say you're a complainer short on material, aided dating will fill the well...forever.

Benefit No. 5

Sometimes Internet dating actually leads to a date you want to go on! Wow!!

It's the human condition to want to be part of a union. Yearning for a mate is part of the drive that gets you one. It makes you shower, put on makeup, keep a trim figure, dress nicely, and suffer through laser hair removal. Note to all the feminists out there: of course we do these things for ourselves, but getting some scooty out of the deal isn't a bad reward, is it?

Should you meet many males—some upstanding, some just standing up—and there's no spark, don't fret. Merely keep in mind that dating is a:

* long-distance marathon that requires perseverance and a long-term outlook
* numbers game: you just need one ('til you get divorced, then you just need one more). And that one could be lurking behind your very next click and for that fact alone, it's all worth it.

Hairball

Miami Soul Machine Finds London Matey on the Internet

Dear Laurie,

About six months ago, I met a wonderful guy online. We hit it off right from the start and talked every day for hours. I met him a couple of months ago and we had the same chemistry in person as we did online. I plan to visit him in December. Then in February, he will be visiting me. We are very much in love and feel we have found our soulmates. The problem is that he lives in London and I live in Miami. We are thinking of getting a fiancé visa and getting married so we can be together. I really feel I can spend the rest of my life with this man. Can this really work?

Missing My Other Half

Dear "Other Half,"

Congrats on meeting a guy who makes you swoon. What a great feeling. Yay, fun, whoop de whoop. Sha na na, etc., etc. I am of four minds on this one.

Mind 1: *Carpe Diem* (that's Latin for "scale the fish"). The idea here is that you only live once and if you've never scaled a fish before, well, high time! You're embarking on life-altering (potentially threatening) decisions while at the mercy of your hormones—ahhh, so what! You only live once.

Mind 2: Oh dear God, you foolish fool you. You're making decisions about moving halfway around the world while at the mercy of your hormones. Get a hold of yourself. Go directly to some form of sanity—do not pass go, do not collect two hundred dollars. Clear your head, cross your legs, then let's talk.

Mind 3: Hold it just one online minute here. Stop the Internet music. What's the big hurry? You just met six measly months ago—that's only two seasons. Don't you know you should at least see how a man dresses through four before embarking on such rash decision-making? How do you know this guy isn't a freak just waiting to happen (not to mention a potential fashion nightmare)? Do you even have any support system once overseas? Oy!

Mind 4: You've met The One. Faaaaaaantastic! And you met him online and he lives halfway around the world. What a great story to tell your grandkids.

I'm going to assume you've had all of these thoughts at one point or another, but want me to play bad cop and set you straight. Okay, I will.

Here are my thoughts on love and distance. Great classics and devastating wars would not have been written or fought throughout history if admiring from afar weren't so much more appealing than relating up close. Ever heard: "Absence makes the heart grow fonder"? Oh yeah, that.

In a nutshell, indications that a relationship is a goner take about four times as long to compute through a long-distance lens and, conversely, all things good get magnified tenfold. Extrapolating further: as the weaker, bad signals take their old, sweet time to hit home, the super-duper, good feelings fly in fast and furiously. Caution: People may appear cooler and more awesome from far away than they actually are in real life (therefore the making of serious, life-altering decisions while under the influence of distance is not recommended).

Then there's the issue of post long distance—or being in the same place. It's next to impossible to maintain the long distance, romantic, wooing levels of emotion and activity once living at a distance is eliminated. Just so you know, there's a period of serious adjustment and, often, letdown. Like it or not, you will have to land at some point.

The short answer: Doom and gloom aside, "Can this really work?" Sure it can, but I would caution you to take your time!! The two of you are veritable strangers. You're willing to uproot your life/get married (!!) over a few months of phone calls and emails and one in-person meeting?! Time to read, For Whom the Clue Phone Rings. If you two are truly soulmates, then taking another six to twelve months to get to know each other's souls better will only enhance your soulful lives. Peace, dudes.

Lovingly&logically yours,
Laurie

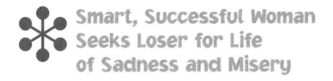

Smart, Successful Woman Seeks Loser for Life of Sadness and Misery

Dear Laurie,

My boyfriend and I have been together for two years—I'm twenty-one, he's twenty-six. When we met, we were both on the same "level," both poor college students just looking for someone to have fun with. Now, I'm making good money while I'm still going to college and waiting patiently for this relationship to progress to something more, while he's dropped out of college, living with his parents because he doesn't make enough money, and dragging his feet when it comes to a commitment to me. I imagine myself spending the rest of my life with this guy (believe me—he does have some good qualities), but why is he acting like our ages are switched? And even more—why doesn't he care that he's not making anything of himself?

Carrie

Dear Carrie,

You don't sound like the buck-toothed, bun-in-the-oven, red-neck type, so what's your marriage hurry at twenty-one? You said yourself, when you went into the dating store, you were "just looking for someone to have fun with" and that's exactly what you came out with. Expecting Fun Model No. 206 to turn into marriage material is a little unrealistic.

Bear with me while I do some math here. Let's see, you're twenty-one now and have been dating the World's Most Ambitious Boyfriend (WMAB) for two years, which makes you—take the square root and carry the two—nineteen when you met. Nineteen! Carrie, that's only two and three quarters in dog years! You're too young to be planning a life with a shmoe. Why not wait at least five more years to funk up your life; give yourself something to look forward to. On the other hand, starting young in the screw-up department has its advantages; you get it out of your system early, you still have time for an epiphany (at, say, twenty-seven or twenty-eight), you can then do a mad dash to get all of your psychological shit together (by, say, thirty-three), meet the man of your healthy dreams (in the produce department of your local supermarket), and live happily ever after.

"Believe me—he does have some good qualities."

I'm trying to think what qualities would override what you've already told me. I'm trying to think what you could tell me that would convince me to cross out everything I've written thus far and stand up and cry, "Carrie may have her sights set on a loser, but he is a very special loser. Hallelujah and praise the Lord!"

"...why is he acting like our ages are switched?"

First of all, in terms of relative maturity, a twenty-six-year-old male is the equivalent of a twenty-one-year-old female (if he's at all lucky). I have a whole theory on maturity, which I will now elucidate for you. While it's true size matters, age, on the other hand, does not. We are each born with what I call a Maturity Achievement Center that is preprogrammed at birth to reach and not exceed a specified level—regardless of input.

Carrie, when you met the WMAB, you and he were at the same level of maturity—his maturity center having already achieved maximum full-throttle potential while yours was just kicking in. As you were preparing for takeoff, he was negotiating how best to avoid a crash landing.

The short answer: Alas, I have once again reached the end of another sheet of paper, which is my cue to shut up. I leave you with this: in my opinion, if you push hard enough, your college-dropout, live-at-home, commitment-phobic, pauper-of-a-boyfriend will marry you (I guarantee it) and then you'll be the lucky owner of a slightly used college-dropout, live-in-your-home, commitment-phobic (he'll find other things to drag his feet on, believe me) pauper-of-a-husband. Congratulations and good luck.

Lovingly&logically yours,
Laurie

Dear Laurie,

My boyfriend and I have been together for sixteen and a half months. Sometimes we talk dirty to each other. He is more experienced than I. I don't know what to tell him during phone sex. I never know what to say that will compensate for the dirty things he says to me. Any suggestions?

Ms. L

Dear "Ms. L,"

"Give a girl a dirty-talk speech and she'll sound like a broken record. Teach a girl to dirty talk and she'll never be at a loss for nasty words..."

When one needs to conduct serious dirty-talk research in under fifteen minutes, where better to turn for enlightenment than the World Wide Web? More specifically, after typing "sex chat room," I dialed up the AAA Free Sex chat room where I met the likes of Nasty Slut, KingLionHeart, Spanky, Private Duty Nurse, Throbbing Squirtgun, Oliver Clothesoff, Lady Licks-It-

Clean, and Ms. Sweetlips. I, who have never done this before, of course, (scout's honor, but I do sincerely thank Miss L for this "research assignment") was HotnJuicy. AAA seemed a good safe place for a first-timer like myself. It was quite easy to slide into the queue and get a rap going.

Oh, my God—let me tell you—there is no better way (and, trust me, you don't know what I'm about to say here) to try your hand at verbal seduction than in a safe, anonymous environment as the Web. Of course, translating this same freedom to someone you have to look in the eye come morning casts a slightly different light on the story, but that mere detail needn't stop you from giving it a whirl!

From what I've gathered over the years, through this column and at AAA, the No. 1 guy turn-ons that Miss L might want to touch on include:

A. Guys like to know their Johnsons are BIG!
B. Guys like to know their Johnsons are BIG! and that you want their BIG! Johnsons morning, noon, and night, including mid-morning as well as early evening.
C. And these BIG!-Johnson guys want to know you want them in whatever manner they wish to give it to you, which often is a combination of the upside down and backward. And the biggest guy-pleaser is to manage all this with a sweet smile on your face (even if, at that point, they can no longer see your face).

But I pause here because one thing Miss L wrote gave me pause, "The problem is, I never know what to say that will compensate for the dirty things he says to me." Dirty talk is not a tournament where you win a prize or pay someone back. If you mean you're not sure how to turn him on as much as he turns you on, well, then ask him. But if you're saying you're really uncomfortable, then you need to say so and game's over. End of story. Or maybe you realize you need to take it slower. Whatever. It's just the two of you, so develop what-ever ground rules you need to make it a feel-good thing. And have fun!!!

The short answer: Miss L, give yourself the freedom to open up this side of yourself. It may be a little embarrassing at first, but part of the beauty of an intimate relationship is developing the trust to do the different things that makes your relationship special—not all these special things have to revolve around sex, of course, but when they do—yee-haw!

So, practice with the silliness, sexiness, and initial scariness of it all. Ask your lover what he likes to hear—not verbatim— but what topics turn him on. That'll give you a start. If he's turning you on and you gain more confidence about turning him on, the whole thing should start to build into this hot, throbbing...well, you get the picture.

Lovingly&logically yours,
Laurie

Dear Laurie,

I am a fifty-eight-year-old woman who is married to a sixty-eight-year-old man. He is a good man and we have been married for forty-two years, but our sex life is nil and I am a very passionate woman who has needs. My dilemma is this: I have met this other man on the Internet who I really care about. We have never met and I have tried to cut it off with him, but it leaves me in tears for days. Is there something wrong with me? We have verbal sex on the Internet and it is wonderful and he tells me he is even more wonderful in person. Don't know what I should do—stay with the one I married who is good to me in other ways or go with the one that fulfills my fantasies as a lover? He, too, is wonderful and very caring, tender, loving, romantic, and sexual in all the ways I desire.

What to Do?

Dear "What-to-Do-to-Whom,"

Life sure was a lot simpler a few short decades ago, I tell you. It was an innocent time when horny wives simply banged the milkman and then went about cleaning house. And horny men? Well, since time immemorial, they simply bent a secretary or two over the desk and that was that. There was none of this should-I-leave-my-wife/husband for a good lay—not a lot of it that was serious, anyway. People didn't leave their husbands/wives for mistresses (and mister-esses) for a variety of reasons—the biggest one being that you'd have to stop calling them "mistresses." And no one likes a name change mid-story—it's very confusing.

Okay, so sex is nonexistent for this "very passionate woman who has needs." Amen to women's needs and knowing you have them. I hear you, but why all of a sudden—after forty-two years of marriage—are you up in arms about your nil sex life? Has it always been nil? Have you ever talked to your husband about these passionate needs? If not, why not? If not, get off the Internet, i.e. fantasy central, and schedule a date with your real, live husband.

If, on the other hand, you have talked about this with your hubby—all to no avail—well, then I do think a Plan B is in order. And Internet man ain't it. Believe me. He is a figment of your imagination. Period. Exclamation point! What man wouldn't want to talk dirty with a woman online? How safe. How easy! What man wouldn't say he's even more wonderful in person? Duh. Even at the wise age of fifty-eight you are currently operating under a (verbal) sex haze. Danger! Danger Will Robinson!

Your current decision-making abilities are about as good as those comatose band members on the *Titanic*.

Wake up and smell the burning reality. Your Internet man is a fantasy and that is all! You've never even met him, for God's sake. So you get off with your keyboard lover—how nice and tidy. You never have to smell his occasionally unpleasant breath or wash any mussed-up sheets. Everything is just cyberperfect! And I'll bet just about anything he wants to keep it that way. You can't be serious, thinking this guy really wants you to leave your husband to start a life with him. Good Lord!

The short answer: Stop getting off on the Internet and just plain get off (i.e. log off). Leave yourself in tears for a few days if you have to—you'll live. You're killing off a fantasy and that's worth a tear or two. Then sit down dry-eyed and clear-headed and ask yourself if you are ready to leave your husband. Are you ready to call it quits without the crotch crutch or the keyboard-equivalent of a talking dildo? Maybe you are. Maybe you aren't. But therein lies the issue. Maybe you're finally waking up to your needs (married at sixteen, for Chrissake!) and the finiteness of your time on this Earth. Maybe this is a gyration you go through every few years. Whatever the case, you've got a tough decision before you, but a decision that deserves to be made with a sound mind and unencumbered vagina. Have courage to realize your full potential, but don't sell yourself short with just any portal in a storm...

Lovingly&logically yours,
Laurie

Saved from the Future Ex
Craig, 38
How We Met: Internet Dating

When Craig picked me up, he brought over a Calla lily plant and a welcome-to-the-neighborhood card. How thoughtful! Too bad he was—how you say—beauty challenged. I wanted to him ask where the guy in the photo he sent me was, but I didn't. While I was eager to deliver the final report, my conclusion would have to wait. Like a sharp pebble grinding its way into the tender arch of your foot, this date would have to run its course, as sometimes irritating pebbles have a way of turning into beautiful pearls right inside your sweaty shoe...that, or an infected abscess treatable with hydrogen peroxide and antibiotics.

We drove to the nearby mall (ack!) and parked across from the Cheesecake Factory (please note: conducting a date in an establishment with the word "cheese" in the title skews an already stacked deck). As we crossed the parking lot, Craig:

❋ told me his "not an intellectual" ex-wife of thirteen years left him for the bouncer at the corner pub

❋ said, "Oh, you're writing a book? Where are you getting your content?" (little did he know what a wealth he would provide); and

❋ used the word, "Rockin'!" a record seventeen times in grammatically correct sentences.

It was then I began executing the near-perfect nod-and-smile. I progressed to clicking my heels together, thinking, "There's no place like not here. There's no place like not here."

When that effort produced less than satisfying results, I experimented with phrases like, "Yes," and "Really?!" sometimes followed up by, "Hmmm."

At this point, I would like to set the scene. Please remember I had been in Craig's presence for a solid half hour already. We had chatted a good deal—enough to know that the plane was going down!

We walked into the restaurant side by side. Grateful to no longer nod sideways, I looked straight ahead at the hostess and said, "Hello."

Craig turned to my ear (since I was focused straight ahead) and with great enthusiasm replied, "HELLO!!"

Okay, that all happened very quickly, so let's rewind and run it again, shall we?

There we are, Craig and I, walking side by side—*mano a mano*, if you will. See me? I'm advancing, now looking straight ahead at the hostess directly in front of me. We make eye contact, the hostess and I. Our eyes lock on. At that very moment, I search (and quickly find) the word to best express my sentiment. I say: "Hello." (The very common, widely used, and well-understood North American speech term used for greeting.) To which Craig enthusiastically replied (into my ear), "HELLO!!"

Were the scene written as stage directions it would look something like this:

Laurie to Hostess: *Hello.*

Craig to Laurie and her left ear: *HELLO!!*

Good-bye.

Ex
Files

seven

Ex Sex:

need I Say More?

Sex with an ex—not to be confused with break-up sex—can be a great way to stay connected to the land of the living while searching for your next true love. First, to clarify, break-up sex is sex right after you've broken up, say within a one- or two-month window. Emotions are running high and hope is springing eternal. Break-up sex is often conducted under the influence of alcohol in the form of a booty call or, innocently enough, after running into each other at a party when you've temporarily forgotten how rude or boring or stingy he is. Like slipping on a banana peel, sex at this point is easy—just a little "whoops" and you're there, which often leads to thoughts of "Reunited and It Feels So Good" by Peaches and Herb, quickly followed by "You're a Dick" by...I forget who wrote that.

For sex with an ex to qualify as such (and not be break-up sex), the two of you need to have been apart for a minimum of eight months or so and have already embarked on a new dating career indicating you are truly exes. The benefits of ex sex are two-fold:

 ❋ it keeps the mojo running, so you're not reeking of desperation as the dateless months tick by; and
 ❋ it's relatively safe...physically, anyway.

Only you can judge if you're emotionally competent to stand an ex-sex trial in bed. If he dumped you—no matter how amicably—be prepared to feel reduced to the lowly life-form/quivering mess you were the first time around. Only this time, it'll be worse, since you were supposedly over him already.

On the other hand, if you're the one who did the breaking up, chances are, sex with your ex will be pretty darn good (if sex was good to begin with, that is).

WARNING: If sex was weird or an "issue" while you were dating, do not, I repeat, do not attempt to engage in sex with your ex! Nothing good comes from revisiting weird issues. And while being really drunk is no excuse for sleeping with your ex (or anyone, for that matter), if you're pondering the proposition, it sure makes the transition a hell of a lot easier.

Bon appetit!

Early Ex

A NEW Boyfriend Is...

...an ex who arrived too early.

Gee, I wonder what that makes a NEW husband...

Dear Laurie,

I am a happily married woman with two beautiful kids by my husband and a son from a prior marriage. We have been together for four years and married for one. We both have good jobs and are getting ready to buy a new home. But there's something wrong because I can't stop thinking about my ex-husband. He is in prison and we write letters back and forth. We are just friends. But there must be something missing from my marriage for me to keep thinking about my ex-husband.

Married, but still in the past.

Dear "Your-Marriage-Will-Soon-*Be*-in-the-Past,"

Your letter is like a David Lynch movie where everything is picture-perfect until you hone in on that pesky bug crawling in the ear of the dead person who lies face up on the perfectly manicured lawn of Suburbia, U.S.A.

Prison, did you say? I had to read that one twice. You snuck it in there so nonchalantly, as if you were saying, "He is in New Jersey or real estate." Now, while I haven't directly experienced dating or marrying an imprisoned man *per se* or having a guy imprisoned during the term of my courtship or marriage, I do have a few thoughts on the matter. It is my understanding that people are imprisoned to keep them out of society. It's an extreme form, granted, with the bars and all, but that's the gist as I recall. And yet you are fantasizing about getting this guy back into society, into your society to be exact, into your kids' society, and possibly into your current husband's society—he'll be happy to hear about that. Maybe the two of you could set aside a room for him in this new house you're buying.

You write: "...there must be something missing from my marriage for me to keep thinking about my ex-husband." Maaaaaybeee, but that sounds slightly un-self-aware, as in maybe there's something missing in you. As in maybe there'd be "something missing" no matter who you were with. By continuing to write "friendly" letters to your imprisoned ex—by putting energy into maintaining that (screwed-up) tie—you are fueling your own destructive fire. Why? That relationship ended at least five years ago. What are you getting out of the connection? I'm assuming your current husband does not know you are pen pal-ing with Clinker Joe. I suggest you keep it that way.

So, the real question is why do you need to keep distance between you and your current husband by fantasizing about the man in the orange jumpsuit (a very "in" color this season, by the way)? Maybe something is missing with your current husband—I don't know, you didn't give me enough informa-tion—but, whatever it might be, if you keep it in the realm of fantasy with your ex and never introduce it into your real, live marriage, your current scenario doesn't have a snowball's chance in hell. For example, perhaps Mr. Incarcerated tells you how beautiful/wonderful/awesome (fill in the blank) you are, while your current hubby is not quite so glib/verbal. You need to tell Free Bird (that'd be your current husband) what you need—give him a chance to stand and deliver. You guys might grow closer by sharing your needs. Maybe then you'd prefer to live in the real world and could give up on the idea that as soon as your jailed ex is sprung life will be great.

The short answer: Honey, deal with what's real. Thank your phenomenally lucky stars that you've had the good sense ('til now) to have an ex who is jailed and a current who is free (and not the other way around). Stop writing to Papillon (great movie—rent it if you haven't seen it). You heard me, stop it. It is foolish, irresponsible, senseless. You are a mother, a role model—what would you tell your kids if they came to you ask-ing for advice about a similar situation?! If he's the father of your child, he has the right to visitations (maybe) and the obli-gation to turn over his license-plate money for child support (I hope), but other than that, you two need to be through! Case dismissed.

Lovingly&logically yours,
Laurie

Once a Cheater, Always a Jerk

Dear Laurie,

Hello, well I'm really confused. Me and my guy went out for about three months and broke up because he cheated on me. Well, we got back together about two months ago (we had been broken up for five months) and everything is going fine. But—thing is—I can't help but feel hurt about the fact that he deceived me. I love him very much and I know he loves me, but I sometimes feel like I can't trust him. I honestly don't think he would do it again but I can't forget it. It still hurts. I guess my question is: Should I trust him and be with him? I'm so confused. Please help.

In Love in Alabama

Dear "'Bama,"

I have a very strict policy on cheating. It's called: Buh-Bye. It's also commonly referred to as: See Ya'. But we're talking about you, not me (damn!).

Even so, Bama-lama, I can't tell you to trust or not trust someone. That would be like me telling you to like algebra or excel at swimming or have blue eyes. I can't tell you how to be. You are who you are, you feel what you feel. But let's pretend for a moment that I am almighty and powerful and can tell you how to be and feel. Many of the people who write in talk to me as if I am anyway, so here goes.

Yes, trust the snake. He very well may never cheat on you again (then again, he very well may, 'cause you certainly didn't expect him to do it the first time). But he's back with you and not with her, right? He said he's sorry, "Oops, sorry." And you don't want to belabor the point, do you? I mean, he might get sick of you dredging up the past, for God's sake, and leave or use that as his new excuse to cheat again. Why not be a good little girl and shut up about your feelings and move past it already?!

Or: no, don't trust him. He cheated on you. He was intimate with another woman behind your back. He could have put or be putting your health at risk. He's lame! A coward! Is excuse-less. And on top of that, pathetic. Like he deserves one iota of your kindness. Leave the slob.

Bama-lama-ding—what does it matter what I say? But, from your note, it sounds like you don't trust him anyway. You write, "...I sometimes feel like I can't trust him." You've already made things easier on me and yourself by telling me how you genuinely feel, so let's go from there, shall we? So, you don't trust the lout (you said so yourself) and who can blame you? But you're not ready to let him go. Why? Oh, the usual—sad about losing what you once thought you had and scared to be alone again. My advice: let yourself suffer/be tormented a little while longer with this mo (a.k.a moron) until you simply can't stand it any longer and then be on your way. Find a man who has the maturity to eat off the plate in front of him first, before rummaging in the back for dessert.

The short answer: Bama-lama-ding-dong, distrust is like rust in winter. It will eat away at the foundation of a relationship lickety-split. On the surface, everything is hunky-dory. But peel away the top layer and it's all rotten underneath. Pretty soon, when you go to put on the brakes, your foot goes right through the floorboard, skidding painfully onto the rushing pavement. Yow!

Lovingly&logically yours,
Laurie

Saved from the Future Ex
Gary, 34
How We Met: At a Fundraiser

When I met Gary, I'd been sexually hibernating for most of the winter, as many women do when "food" sources are scarce. The arrival of spring had awakened the mojo beast in me, so when I met Mr. Jones, I was huuungryyyyy. Hungry Jack!

Gary looked exactly like what he was: a two-timin,' weight-liftin,' light-bulb-beach-goin,' cute-in-a-plastic-way, mental lightweight with a poorly functioning snausage (only I didn't know that last part at the time).

To Gary's credit, he told me he had a girlfriend the night we met. And to my discredit, I didn't care. He'd only been seeing her for about a month and whined about how boring she was. He even went so far as to share with me that she was an "every-thing-but" girl, which, according to his sexual calculations, made him a free agent.

Typically, I stay away from these hairy, convoluted love trysts. They bore me because everyone involved thrives on the drama of it all. To be honest, I was just looking for some lip and wasn't too concerned about how I was going to get it.

When we got back to my place, we walked the dog and had tea. By this time, it was 1:00 AM. I sat on the couch and patted the cushion next to me. He came over and sat down. We stared awkwardly at each other.

"Are you going to kiss me?" I asked.

"No," he said. "I've got a girlfriend."

"Wow, I really respect that," I said. Two minutes later, we were making out and at 3:00 AM, I politely showed him how the front door worked.

We saw each other a couple more times after that, but with each meeting, I grew less and less interested. Aside from eating food and having fingerprints, we shared little else in common. Of course, my disinterest only served to heighten his interest (reconfirming the widely renowned, Love Stinks! theory). And so I kindly but firmly deleted his messages...and him along with them.

−eight−

Ex Ex:

a not-So-Merry Go-Round with Past Loves

this is a situation where you make an ex of an ex. How the game works:

1. You have a boyfriend.

2. The two of you break up (dumping party is irrelevant).

3. The two of you get back together (often on the advice of Jim Beam or his close friend Jack Daniels).

4. Then, just as all your tight-lipped friends predicted (amongst themselves, of course), the two of you break up again (see no. 3).

People break up for a reason—pick a reason, any reason—and when they get back together, that special little reason gets back together with them (hello, reason!). This special reason bugs you (or him) as much as, if not more than, it did the first time, *et voilá*, another break-up is in order. And then don't we all feel silly?

Who are these freaks? Well, I'm a card-carrying member (and I suspect you might be, too). Repeat break-up is initiation into a club you really don't want to be a part of, but sort of can't resist—it's the hope-springs-eternal/loneliness-sucks combo on rye that usually keeps members coming back. Chances are, once you've been inducted into the Ex Ex Club, you ain't coming back to renew your membership anytime soon. Are there slow learners in the crowd? Oh sure, and to make it worth their while, we offer a handsome plastic keychain and fridge magnet as a welcome-back gift to those renewing members.

Are there couples who break up, get back together, and stay together (i.e. get married)? Indeed there are, but long-term, longitudinal studies (that I made up in my head) show they have lousy marriages, produce funked-up kids, and regret the day they were born.

Break-ups are a time for personal reflection and growth. After a short respite, take what you've learned out into the world. Go meet someone fresh and exciting with whom you can create a new set of similar yet slightly different reasons to break up. The possibilities are limitless!

You're a Jerk

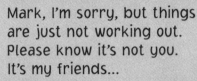

Will Thirty-Eight-Year-Old Mama's Boy Ask Lover to Marry?

Dear Laurie,

My boyfriend and I have been together for ten years. With a promise (from him) to be married some day. Lives with his mom. I have my own home. Oh yeah, he's thirty-eight years old. Any hope of this ever happening?

Mama's Boy Lover-in-Waiting

Dear "Boy Lover,"

I'm sorry, but I call you that because it's what you are: the lover of a boy who, for whatever reason, has not, at the advanced age of thirty-eight, grown into a man. Will he ever? Who knows?! Better question? Who cares?!

For bizarro psychological reasons (that I can only guess at), this guy has never wanted or—thanks to Mom and Mom Jr. (a.k.a. you)—needed to grow up and be an adult. With codependents like you two around, why should he? Who wouldn't want to remain in a permanent state of irresponsibility? Well, most of us, I suppose, but my point is that any latent gumption that Mama's Boy ever had in his reservoirs curled up and died a good, long while ago.

So, he's promised to marry you "some day"?! That's a rich one. He can't even name a decade! No, siree. He gets to keep his anxieties at bay by saying, "some day." And you have accepted that!

I could be wrong (but rarely am). One thing we know for sure—this guy certainly ain't evolving any time soon. Still living with Mom, kept you on a string for ten years (wow), and is approaching forty!! This guy may even be de-volving. If you catch him sucking his thumb, shoot me an email.

Time to turn the spotlight on you, Lover-in-Waiting. I know this sounds harsh, but what's the matter with you that you have hung on to half a man for close to half your life? You obviously don't think you deserve better. Give me one good reason why you don't deserve a guy who can commit to you and offer his hand in marriage in real time? One little reason...I'm waiting. Well, when you come up with it, add it to the bottom of that thumb-sucking email you're going to send me, hmm?

"Any hope of this ever happening?"

Well, it seems we've sort of covered this, but I like to be thorough in my responses. According to Marketing 101: past behavior is the best predictor of future behavior. People change if they want to (not because other people want them to). From your short, sweet note, it seems the only person who may want change would be you. Mama likes her baby boy by her side. Otherwise, she would've heave-hoed him ages ago (mamas are supposed to do that, you know).

The short answer: Assuming you're going to hang around for another decade, here's my suggestion: give Mama's Boy an ultimatum. But if you give an ultimatum, you must be prepared to walk or don't even bother. If you really still want this boy-man, make him set a date, pick a place to have the ceremony, and make him put down a nonrefundable cash deposit (if he has any money, that is). Yeah, he can still back out, but it makes the initial commitment that much more real and palpable. Chances are he'll manage to rationalize his way out of the whole thing, but maybe he'll renew my faith in humanity and rise to the occasion. I wish you luck.

Lovingly&logically yours,
Laurie

Dear Laurie,

About five months ago, my girlfriend of six years broke the relationship off, citing confusion and unsurity about further commitment. I saw her off and on again for about the next two months and then I simply couldn't handle it anymore. I broke off contact and haven't seen much of her since. I saw her recently at a mutual friend's Christmas party and a week later, she called inviting me to a hockey game. Box seats. All expenses paid. The works. On New Year's Eve.

Why would she want to take me, of all people? I have had little to no contact with her and she has a few other people that she could take besides me. Is this the first step in reconciliation or is it simply a nice thing to do? I don't want to get hurt again, but this whole thing has given me a lot of potentially false hope.

Utterly Confused

Dear "Utterly Used,"

Six years! Wow. I first read six months and thought, "Oh B.F.D., I've got bigger woes to fry." But upon closer examination...well, I've got it now. So, she broke off the relationship, "citing confusion and unsurity about further commitment," eh? Did she cite the statute in its entirety or just paragraph three? And one more thing—did she have a lawyer present? Because if she didn't, that could change everything.

What is up with not knowing how you feel about someone after six years? That's 2,190 days or 52,560 hours or 3,153,600 minutes. If someone was patient enough to give me three million-plus minutes to figure out how I felt about something, I'd come up with a pretty solid answer.

Please prepare yourself for the thirty-foot tsunami that's coming in because I'm about to lay it on the line for you, mister. Ambivalence is an answer. The fact that your girlfriend can't say she unequivocally wants to be with you after six years is answer enough. I know you're busy doing the achy-breaky-heart dance right now (extended mix), but harboring hopes of reconciliation will only prolong it. So she runs into you and offers a last-minute invite?!?!?!? What a princess! You know what you can tell her to do with her box and her seats? Have a little pride, bud. Tell her you've got better things to do, like clip your toenails or scrub the soap scum from your tub!

This woman obviously has strong feelings for you or she wouldn't have spent six years with you. Naturally, she misses you. Adjusting to being alone is scary and next to impossible after such a long relationship. Seeing you at this party after being apart jump-starts all sorts of hopes, fantasies, and "if onlys." I'm sure her efforts—to some degree—are based on genuine feeling, but, for the most part, I'd be very suspicious (oh, and good luck reestablishing any trust you once had). She's a girl on the rebound and she's going to bounce whoever crosses her path. And if you go sit in her box, well, she's going to bounce you. Don't get me wrong—chances are great that the two of you will fall back into coupledom for two or four or six months, but mark my LoveLogic words: it won't work out for good. Sorry. (But—you could have some awesome break-up sex.)

Now, this is the part where I slap you around a bit (more). If your lover no longer wants to be with you, hey, free country, right? But for her to stand on one foot, then the other, and ask you to live in the shadow of a falling hammer—hey, that's thoughtless and mean and puts you in the world's biggest no-win position. You can:

* lie down and let her ambivalently walk all over you as she tries to figure herself out, or...
* get angry (a natural response to feeling rejected), but she'll just use that as an excuse to make up her mind and leave, or...
* bend over backward and try to be the most perfect, bestest boyfriend—hoping she'll wake up one day and realize how much she really loves you, or, or, or...get my drift?

The kinder, gentler, more adult approach would have been for her to make an independent decision (one that does not require you to stand by and experience the emotional equivalent of a sharp stick in the eye) and tell you things aren't working/not sure why/good-bye (time-lapse writing).

The short answer: You're sad. You feel terribly rejected. The quickest way to (temporarily) stem this gut-wrenching heartache is to get back together. Well...wake up! You've already invested six years. If you guys were meant to be together, you'd be together already—committed, married, etc. I know it's hard to make sense of it all right now, but, like it or not, it is time to move along. Nothing to see here. Go ahead and spend New Year's Eve with Miss Iffy—pick off that scab. Pick it good. When you're finally sick of her shenanigans, you'll have plenty of time to grow a new one.

Lovingly&logically yours,
Laurie

Saved from the Future Ex
Brett No-Phone Schmitt, 31
How We Met: Workshop

I met Brett at a two-day filmmaking seminar. He sat in front of me and, as the four-foot-three-inch, ascot-sporting teacher yelled for eight hours, I mentally escaped and found inner peace by staring at Brett's broad and muscular back.

Over lunch, I managed to finagle Brett's email address out of him. He supposedly worked at a big, corporate law firm—or at least his email address did. I wrote him and he quickly wrote back:

"I never got to hear much about your 'creative endeavors'— if you have the time, let's meet up and talk. If you're ever in the downtown area during the weekdays, we could 'do lunch'..."

Well, bingo! It just so happened I had one opening for a broad-backed cutie in my schedule! But wait—do you recall that in paragraph two I wrote, "big, corporate law firm address"? I wrote it to let you know that to the best of my knowledge, Brett worked (or at the very least, received email) at a big, corporate law firm. Last I checked, law firms are sub-scribers to the Ma Bell system...and yet he writes:

"...am currently without phone (long story), so if you give me your phone number, I'll try to get hold of you sometime this weekend..."

For those of you who don't speak "boy," let me translate:

"...am currently without phone..." conveys variable information depending on the intonation of the phrase. The fol-lowing two meanings can be inferred:

1. Please don't call me at home, my girlfriend might answer.
2. I'm a deadbeat with no credit, no heat, no electricity, no subscription to *Men's Health*, no phone.

"…(long story)…" means this is embarrassing, please don't ask (these are the stories I pursue most vigorously).

"…I'll try to get hold of you…" With the near-ubiquitous availability of cell and pay phones (and let's not forget big, corporate law firm phones), I applaud Brett for agreeing to try. But let's face it, for whatever reason, this guy had no phone and so for a variation on that reason…he never called.

nine

Ex Engaged:

HE's Moved on to Ruin Someone Else's Life...Forever

years have passed since your ex kissed you in the morning and then just walked away. You've played your Gloria Gaynor CD so many times it's warped. All in all, you have, indeed, survived! You have moved on emotionally, sexually, psychically, spiritually, organically, and yet...

And yet when a friend calls to tell you he's engaged, that he actually got his act together enough to buy the ring and eek out the words, you are stunned—simply and utterly. And while, on some level, you know this poor woman must have done some bad shit in a former life to deserve the likes of him, you still feel your tuna sandwich heading north to greet you.

"Huh?" you hear yourself say and, "Reeeeally?" along with, "You don't say." And even though you begged yourself not to, you ask questions that make it look like you care (because you do), including: "When are they are getting married?," "How big is the ring?" and worst of all, "Would you say she's, uh, prettier than I am?" New lows—once considered theoretically impossible—have been established.

OH DEAR GOD WHY?!

Hearing about your ex getting engaged is:

A. your worst fear come to life (and if it wasn't clear before, let it be clear now that your main purpose on this planet is to stylishly take all the shit life has to throw at you), and

B. not the way you expected it to turn out.

You were supposed to get married first! You were going to fall madly and immediately in love with Mr. Tall, Dark, and Handsome, "accidentally" run into your ex while sporting your princess-cut, two-carat diamond and revel in seeing, and later hearing, how distraught he was upon receiving "the news" (but that's you instead, oops).

When he dumped you, you thought: "Just give me a moment to wash this asshole right out of my bouffant 'do and then I's a gonna find me my man!" Right? No, not right. Not right at all! In fact, before you had a chance even to wash him out of your sheets, he was poking the local trash heap. He was! Echoes of "yippy ki-yo ki-yay" wafted across town into your bedroom window, he was so indiscreet. Ah well, nothing illegal about that, you suppose. But still.

You sort of half expected and hoped for his—oh, how you say?—dick to get knocked in the dirt. That's right, a little comeuppance. Something to keep your nonreligious faith alive in the natural order of things: that when all is said and done, trash-pokers finish last. Well, it's my personal belief that if you can hang in long enough, you will indeed witness the demise of everyone who has wronged you. I do! But do you want to is the question. Not to get all, "he ain't heavy" on you, but is time spent wishing ill on someone time well spent? If you're an excellent multitasker, maybe—but for the majority of us, the final answer would be "no."

I'm no moral-majority freak and you won't find a "Dog Is My Copilot" bumper sticker on my car, but I do believe:

* negative mental twirlsies wreak havoc over time;
* good things come to those who wait;
* she's not prettier than you;
* there's something to be said for good karma (if only to aid in finding parking).

Getting Married

Dear Laurie,

My boyfriend and I have been together for two and a half years. He has never cheated on me. Now he just left for college to play football. Do you know what he's going to do? Should I trust him? Or not?

"Now he just left for college to play football. Do you know what he's going to do?"

According to the little I know, I believe your boyfriend is going to put on a tight-fitting, hot, and bulky outfit (for protection, mainly, but also to make his butt look good to other players so they'll swat it when a particularly excellent play is made). He'll get knocked around a lot, depending on how fast he is, and maybe lose a few IQ points by the end of the season. But what he loses in intellectual capacity he'll more than make up for in popularity by being on the football team, which brings us to the heart of your real question: "Should I trust him?"

If your boyfriend is trustworthy, you should trust him. The fact that you're asking if you should trust him makes me think he's not ranking high on the trustworthy scale and, therefore, you've answered your own question without even trying. Truth be told (and I don't have the statistics on this one), when people go off to college they change a lot, their eyes get opened to new things and new people, and, yes, typically, previous relationships go by the wayside. I doubt this is what you want to hear, but I gots to tells it like it is. Don't worry, it will happen to you when you go off to college.

The short answer: If you two are truly meant to be together, then you will be. Otherwise, let nature takes its course, while your boyfriend takes his.

Lovingly&logically yours,
Laurie

Absence Makes the Lonely Heart Grow...Weaker

Dear Laurie,

Please feel free to be honest with your opinion. I dated a person for three years and we broke up last year for several reasons. I got tired of being his mother (cooking and cleaning and taking care of him). So, he moves out of state and I tell him I don't care ever to talk to him again.

Well, I haven't dated anyone since him and I wrote him an email a month ago to see how he is. He says he misses me a lot and wants to see me. He is trying to get a ticket to fly and visit me. Do you think what I am feeling is just because I haven't had anyone in my life since him and I am lonely? I think I feel something for him, but how do I know it's going to work out this time? He seems a little more grown up. Am I being stupid again and letting loneliness rule my life? Thanks!

Dear "His Mother,"

Oh, no! You're like the character in the spooky movie who, after seeing the trail of blood, proceeds to venture into the dark and scary room all by herself. Audience members curl in on themselves and hold hands while screaming, "No, don't do it," or "Ohh, I can't believe she's..." Others remain silent, but close their eyes to the impending slaughter. Play *Psycho* shower scene music here because, honey, you are going down!

"Please feel free to be honest with your opinion." Thank you, I will.

People break up for a reason. Ten times out of ten, when they get back together, that reason is still there. Hello, little reason. Oh sure, it may take a while for that reason to reemerge, but trust me, it always does. Would someone please embroider this on a hanky, silkscreen it on a T-shirt, make a bumper sticker out of it, for God's sake—people forget so quickly!

"Do you think what I am feeling is just because I haven't had anyone in my life since him and I am lonely?"

And Bingo was his name-o. Three years is a long time to cook, clean, and take care of someone. Now that Baby Hughey is gone, there is a void and you probably have a lot of free time to fill. When we have a lot of free time, we obsess and roll tape on unfinished business. And when we've exhausted ourselves with this emotional scrutiny and feel crummy, we...email our exes!

"I think I feel something for him, but how do I know it's going to work out this time?"

This is a two-parter. Part one: "I think I feel something for him."

Okay now, this phrase makes me think of being "sort of pregnant." You spent three years with this guy and you think you may be having a feeling? Thinking you have feelings for a (lousy) ex when you're lonely is like having phantom pain from a cut-off limb: it's all in your head.

Part two: "...how do I know it's going to work out this time?"

Because you're going to avoid him like the plague. As far as him seeming more grown up, don't you know everyone looks more grown up from afar? It's an optical illusion that has to do with vanishing-point perspective—let's leave it at that, hmm?

"Am I being stupid again and letting loneliness rule my life?"

Unfortunately, yes. Sisterhood moment: Honey, I'm sorry you're feeling lonely. It is completely understandable. Three years is a long time to spend with someone, whether it was a good three years or not. These things take time to heal and by bringing this guy back in, you're just setting the clock back to zero.

The short answer: The next time you feel yourself missing your out-of-state slob, why not get in touch by doing a load of laundry, washing the dishes, maybe making the bed, or vacuuming? And be glad he's not there to mess up your life all over again.

Lovingly&logically yours,
Laurie

Saved from the Future Ex
Mike, 26
How We Met: Friend of a Friend
(Some Friend!)

I am in Mike's apartment. We are pretending to watch TV, as if the last thing on our minds was the bedroom. Mike sells chatchkes (promotional items you covet at a trade show because they're free). Mike convinces nervous marketing managers to silkscreen their company's name on hundreds of rubberband balls, wrist rests, and solar-powered calculators because how else are they going to affect sales?

Mike is going on about a potential deal with Pepsi and I am pretending to listen, even going so far as to ask interested questions because I'm still not sure if Mike is a temporary or longer-term thing. In the event he becomes the latter, I want to lay the groundwork for appearing to be a caring, attentive girlfriend so I can slack off later.

There we are, watching TV, having pretend conversation, when the phone rings. On the fourth ring, the answering machine picks up. Simultaneously, but not coincidentally, as the machine clicks "on," the TV volume rises. I look over to see Mike maniacally pressing the volume button on the remote control.

I look at him quizzically, coyly, smiling—remember, I am still hedging my potential long-term bet—and point to my ears as he tosses the remote onto the couch, leapfrogs over the sofa, and quickly hits "stop" on the answering machine, but not before I hear a high-pitched woman's voice pleading on the other end: "Mike? Mike, are you there? Mike, if you're there please pick up the phone. Mi…"

It's then I know this is not only not a long-term thing, it's not even a thing. And so we proceed directly to the bedroom.

ten

Pre Ex:

Selling Your "Previously Owned" Boyfriend

If you don't love something,
set it free.
If it comes back,
pawn it off on someone else.

The following concept, borrowed from the highly respectable realm of the used car salesman, is designed to create a kinder, gentler, perhaps less guilty, nation of exes. Imagine if, prior to pink-slipping that special someone, you were required to find your previously owned boyfriend a new "owner," so to speak.

Before purchasing a new car, you find a home for your old car. Maybe you sell it privately, get reamed on a dealer trade-in, possibly even donate it for free—any which way, you are responsible for taking care if its reincarnation. Why not the same for loved ones?

Let's walk through the scenario, shall we? You've had your boyfriend for a good, long while—or it seems good and long to you (time is relative, don't forget). Is his mileage too high and beginning to show? Has a small defect, once nearly undetectable, grown larger and become intolerable? Perhaps you've changed and the features he originally came with no longer fulfill your needs. Maybe it's a simple case of needing to be footloose and wheel-free for a while. Whatever the reason, it's time to trade up.

Step 1: Tidy up your existing boyfriend for sale.

While everyone rationally knows that what's on the inside ultimately matters most, statistics show cosmetic appeal counts for 80 percent of resale value. Your outgoing boyfriend needs to look his best as you shop him around. How to accomplish this without raising suspicion on his part? Flattery! Every time your boyfriend gussies up or looks slightly better than usual, pay him a compliment. Before you know it, he'll be looking so dapper you may reconsider putting him up on the auction block.

Step 2: Place an ad.

So you're ready to compassionately sell, but where are the buyers? All around you! Simply get the word out and let the rest take care of itself. Start by telling two friends. They'll each tell two friends and so on and so on (don't worry about your boyfriend finding out—they're always the last to know). Before you know it, you'll have several quality referrals.

Step 3: Throw a "used-car" party.

Invite a variety of buyers and sellers. This gathering gives potential buyers a chance to look at the goods under non-threatening, socially lubricated circumstances. It also allows others to sell and provides the opportunity for you to discreetly shop, should you be in the market.

Step 4: Drive yourself happy.

Congratulations, you found a buyer—someone who will regularly change his oil and keep him running smoothly. You are now free to pick up your new "set of wheels" (is he foreign? domestic?) or leisurely shop around while luxuriating in your newfound freedom. Road trip!

Dickwad

Dawn, tell me what you think of my ad: "Bitter, white female in search of single, white male who's not a dickwad and enjoys...

Hmm, Marcy, I think "dickwad" is a little strong. How about "jerk-off" instead?

Someday my dickwad will come!

'Scuse Me, While I French Kiss This Guy

Dear Laurie,

Okay, so I've been wondering this: what is the best way to French kiss a guy?

A Confused Girl

Dear "Confused Girl,"

You are to be commended for your inquiry. If only more people of kissing age showed equal concern for proper technique. While personal preference plays a big role in giving and receiving good lip, there are a few kissing dos and don'ts.

1. **Don't** be the tongue that ate New York. Lips protect the entrance of your mouth for a reason. They keep a check on what's buzzing around, what should go in, and, more importantly, what should stay out. Should a heat-seeking tongue missile knock directly on lip's door, I advise you to flatly deny entry.

   You know how when you're about to go swimming you test the water by dipping your toe in the pool? Same idea with French kissing. Start with a little lip-only kissing and then take your tongue and gently, quickly dip it in the pool. Typically, your partner will then dip his or her tongue in your pool. Oh, the water's fine? Jump in for a short swim. Then jump back out. Towel off. Hot again? Dive back in a little deeper. Get refreshed! Go to the bottom. Rest on the side. Practice your flutter kick. Try a little water ballet. The possibilities are endless.

2. **Do** initially keep your lips together. During warm-up, it's easy to get lost in a full-on, total open mouth, but just as you sit in a dress with your knees touching (unless you're doing the hoecake shuffle) so, too, do you begin a kissing session with your lips together. It's less expectant, less come-and-get-me, less desperate. Also, the physical tension, i.e. lip muscles pressing on another's lips, feels pretty gosh darn good. This sort of gives you an outline to follow. Of course, once things get going, lips, among other things, will open up....

3. **Don't** be a spitty slob. There are not many worse things on this Earth than kissing a drooler. Dance cards get very empty very fast if you can't keep your spit to yourself. What to do? I can't exactly describe it, but spit management is akin to the suction device that dentists use to keep saliva levels under control. Using your tongue, sweep excess accumulation to the back where the throat gnome takes over by signaling the esophagus troll to swallow. The swallow flunky then notifies the stomach wombat that a delivery is coming.

4. **Do** take a breather. Kissing is an ebb-and-flow thing (see No. 1). When developing an all-around, strategic-kissing plan, upper-body parts like the neck, earlobes, collarbone, and eyelids should be considered. And, of course, there are many other sensual body parts that require kissing to grow big and strong, but that's probably best left for Kissing Part Deux.

5. **Don't** expect a bad kisser to be any different (i.e. better) in bed. Just as handholding is the prelude to a kiss, kissing is the prelude to a whole lot more. If someone's a bad kisser, you can bet your bottom dollar they'll suck (or be equally unsatisfying) in every other department. Could I be wrong? Sure. Am I? No.

The short answer: Kissing...ahhh, mmm, ohhh! Nothing's better than a long make-out session with a great kisser. And most of my girlfriends agree. "Does he give good lip?" is high on the list when evaluating a potential mate, temporary or otherwise. If you're passionate and interested, chances are you will kiss well, but unless someone tells you, how do you know? If you have courage, you can always ask your kissmate. Or maybe you have a few suggestions yourself. Whether giving or receiving, be kind and compassionate.

So, kiss early, kiss often, and above all: practice, practice, practice.

Lovingly&logically yours,
Laurie

Just Say "No" to Fat Boyfriends in China

Hi Laurie,

I've got a boyfriend now. I know he's a good guy—responsible, cares about me, tolerant, etc. But I just can't have a feeling about him. On the other hand, people say, "You're twenty-eight already, it's time to get married." You know when people say this on and on and on, you start to believe it. But I just don't want to get married, at least not for the moment.

Actually, I am not satisfied with his figure. He's a little bit overweight and my favorite is that kind of guy with a moderate figure. I know it doesn't sound like a reasonable excuse—people always say the most important thing is people's inside rather than outside. I understand that, but still, I don't have any "desire" about him. Is it normal? Anything I can do to improve this situation? In fact, I think he's a good candidate to be a husband, but not the one to be the ideal lover. Looking forward to your comment on this. I believe your input will be enlightening for me. Thanks.

Christine in China

Hello "Christine in China!"

When I'm on a date, if I'm having a decent time of it (i.e. engaged and engaging in interesting/funny/fun conversation), I ask myself, "Hey, Laurie, would you like to lean over the table and kiss the sky, I mean, this guy?" And if I think, "Yeah, you know, I really would," then I figure I'm having a pretty decent time of it and will sign on for the extended plan, i.e. proceed to date number two.

Whether I go on another date again is not the point. The point is do I want to? And the point for you, my dear Christine, is the same. Aside from everyone else's unasked-for opinion, what do you want to do? How do you feel?

"I know it doesn't sound like a reasonable excuse—people always say the most important thing is people's inside rather than outside."

You can't hear me right now, but I'm pretending to cough and mixed in with this fake coughing sound, I'm saying "bullshit" under my breath (don't know the equivalent in Chinese...).

Christine in China, listen up: It's your life we're talking about here. If you're set on a path of misery and sadness, then by all means listen to everyone else and marry your man of immoderate figure! On the other hand, if you value yourself and trust your instincts, then tell your good candidate boyfriend as kindly as you can that you have enjoyed your experiences with him but it is time to move on.

"...I think he's a good candidate to be a husband, but not the one to be the ideal lover."

Christine, love is not a job interview. It's a matter of the heart and head. If all your friends think it's time to get married, well, who's stopping them?! And if they think Mr. Pudge will do, sounds like he's about to be available!

"Anything I can do to improve this situation?"

Yeah, get out.

The short answer: Every happily married person I've ever talked to said they knew pretty quickly their mate was The One. It was a gut reaction that just felt right. Now this "right" person may still do things that bug the living hell out of you, but you can accept those hell-bugging parts because the other 80 percent is A-okay. Christine, it doesn't sound to me like you have the other 80 percent or 50 percent or, well, you get the picture. What you have is a deal-breaker. If he were superb in every other way and was still overweight, could you get over it? Maybe. But maybe not and that's okay, too.

I find that each boyfriend teaches us something invaluable for our next relationship. In this case, you've learned to trust your moderate gut and shy away from others' overweight ones.

Lovingly&logically yours,
Laurie

eleven

Never Ex:

A Fake Boyfriend Is a Must-Have

I have a long-distance boyfriend—or so I told the creep down the street. I pass his house (the creep's) occasionally on afternoon dog walks. That's how he asked me out. To his church social. On Broadway and Market. That night. In front of his ex-wife. And their five-year-old daughter.

It was then I remembered I have a fake boyfriend, so I said, "I'd love to go, but I can't. You see I have a...boyfriend in...San Francisco! Yeah. He's six-feet-one-inch tall. Has brown hair and blue eyes. A former-model-turned-astrophysicist, movie producer, speaks four languages, and likes...disco music."

At times like these, when my fake boyfriend comes to save the day, I begin to wonder: "Just what are we up to these days, my fake boyfriend and I?" I assume we're silly with love. Recently returned from the land of hot and steamy. Temporarily poisoned with a weekend's perfection. I mean, why not? It's my fake boyfriend, after all. Then I think: "Oh my God! Is my fake boyfriend...The (fake) One?"

A long and slippery grin slides across my face as I contemplate the possibility. Stars—no, hearts!—shoot from my sparkly eyes. Languidly I walk, allowing the dog to sniff and trail behind me. Thinking about my unioned future with Mr. Fake-but-Perfect sends shivers of ecstatic...pain, sweet pain as I trip and fall over a tree branch on the sidewalk. "Ahhh!" I skid to a stop on hands and knees against the cement below.

Where is he now, that fake boyfriend of mine, I think as I inspect my torn skin and bruised ego. San Francisco, yeah right. My (real) dog trots over to offer solace and lick my wounds. Together, we eye my scraped knees and sit for a moment.

"Are you okay?" I look up. A handsome stranger bends down to lend a hand. "Professional gravity-tester? Here, let me help you," he says.

"Oh, thanks," I say, taking his (ring-free!) hand. "I think from my landing you can tell I'm no professional," I say, brushing off my skirt, "but nice of you to say so."

Turns out, this gentleman just happens to be going my way. For the next few blocks or so, we chat about all sorts of things including the benefits of listening to disco music while designing rocket engines and writing screenplays.

Set Him Free

Woman Seeks Humorous, Self-Help Book to Retain Man of Her Dreams

Dear Laurie,

I am a forty-two-year-old woman who has just met the man of her dreams—only he lives three hours away. It started off emailing and he came down this weekend and wow—instant, deep chemistry for the both of us.

This distance thing can get very negative and the phone conversations can revolve around missing each other. What can I do for fun, laughter—lots of laughter—to get us through the week or two we can't see each other? He even mentioned my humor snagged him, but I need major help for this one. Any book or Internet sites for recommendations?

Dear "Forty-Two-Year-Old Woman Who
Has Just Met the Man of her Dreams,"

I am happy for you, seriously. "Yay!" You've met someone who floats your boat instantly and deeply. Not an easy feat. And via the Internet, no less. And he's not a freak. Wow. I knew a woman, who shall remain nameless, who waited 'til she was forty-three to get married for the first time—a very sweet, somewhat naïve, not-the-sharpest-spoon-in-the-drawer-type woman and the guy she married was/is a slimeball loser. No need to wait forty-three years for that—you can meet and marry one of those anytime, day or night. Operators are standing by.

"Forty-Two," in my humble opinion, you do not need a joke book to keep this relationship afloat telephonically. No, ma'am, you don't. What you do need is to chill. Remember: desperation reeks like bad perfume and I can smell yours all the way through the Internet via the LoveLogic email portal. Let me explain.

You're forty-two. You've just met a guy you dig. The chances of these two things occurring simultaneously has forced you to rethink the existence of God. Your friends and coworkers enjoy your company again and your mother is shopping for her mother-of-the-bride dress. Or maybe not. But my point is: life is good. Having a man you're jazzed about livens things up. Forces you to dust off feelings you haven't had for a while—feelings you're afraid you might have to, just as quickly, put back into storage. The second-best advice I have for you right now is to relax. And the best advice is this: remember who you are.

Remember all the great, wonderful qualities you have built up on your own over the years. Your genuine you-ness is what attracted this guy to you in the first place and it's what will keep him attracted to you in the long run—not you trying to be you. You sound a little scared, a bit freaked-out right now. Sure, you could read twenty-six self-help books or write in to an online column for random advice (oh, wait, you already did...), but that would be the outside world telling you what to do. Right now, you need to reacquaint yourself with you. Get some of your confidence back. Plant your feet on the ground. Go inside. Get quiet with your bad self. Remember how cool you are. Calm down.

Have you had enough of the new age, some-of-my-best-friends-are-Dalai-Lamas speech? Some practical tactical advice for "Forty-Two."

Cool it. Resist the urge to whine on the phone. Whining is dull. Whining is boring. Whining gets you fed and your diapers changed for the first three years of your life and then it's one of those evolutionary traits that's supposed to disappear like a monkey tail or (with the exception of special times) like walking on all fours.

Think of three positive things you can talk about before you get on the phone with swoon-man. And then talk about those things. If you feel yourself about to tell him you miss him, pinch your earlobe, literally bite your tongue, squeeze your butt cheeks together—I don't care. Anything to distract yourself. Just don't go down the miss-you road. You know where it leads. Be sincere and real, but don't derail by taking highway off-ramps that lead to Negative-ville. Until you all can see each other in the flesh again, get on the happy toll road of phone life and drive, drive, drive.

The short answer: All relationships weather weird crap in the beginning. You two have your own unique set o' weirdo circumstances due to distance. New couples either think the weirdness is worth wading through and hang in or they don't, but trying to buck the system with a quick-fix self-help book/Internet site ain't going to do the trick. If your mate wanted to date a book or an Internet site, he would (and his phone bills would be cheaper). So you're feeling funky—hold on 'til the real you returns. Have a séance to bring her back if she stays away too long. And, whatever you do, don't try to be funny. Please don't try to be funny. Please, pleeease don't try to be funny. Trying to be funny is like a woman trying to have an orgasm—it never happens.

Lovingly&logically yours,
Laurie

Is Girl Crazy for Being Attracted to a Drifter?

Dear Laurie,

My question is: I am very attracted to a man who is a drifter. He lives in a camper, works odd jobs, and goes away to plant trees from December—April every year. But he's so funny, sweet, smart, and sexy. Am I crazy? Thanks!

Dear "Crazy Thanks!,

My knee-jerk reaction was to pretend I was your mother. I thought, "*Oy vaysmeer*, my daughter is dating a drifter. My baby *yegala*" (there's some Yiddish word that sounds like that and I thought it would sound good here). Then I thought, no one writes into LoveLogic to get their mother's opinion; they write to their mothers for that (or not).

Then I pretended I was your good friend who hadn't seen you in a couple of years and we were corresponding by email. This made me think, "What's happened to poor Rita or 'Crazy Thanks!' or whatever your real name is? She used to be so responsible, so levelheaded. Last I heard, she was diligently working her way up the local chapter of Planned Parenthood, volunteering for the blind every Sunday, baking her own fresh blackberry pies…" Then I realized I'd been sucked down a moral majority portal and shook myself like a dog.

I guess the bottom line, "Crazy Thanks!", is this: If you're really connecting from May–November with odd-man-out, then perhaps you need to pursue the potential. Finding a real connection is rare-a-rare-O, so snag it when you can. But make sure that's what you're pursuing and not some souped-up fantasy woven in La-La-Land. Drifters drift for a reason; they no longer want to be part of society or play by the general rules. That could get old after a while, but maybe right now it's different enough to be appealing.

On a more practical side, you said he leaves for half the year, right? If you two fell in love, would he stop his tree-planting ways and make an honest woman out of you? (Where in the world do you find a funny-sweet-smart-sexy camper, odd-job man who plants trees five months a year anyway? While you're on your way to Grandma's house? Looking for the three little pigs? In the yellow pages? My God, you are resourceful.)

The short answer: Truth be told, I've got a bad ju-ju gut reaction about drifter-boy and your enamoration with him (yes, that's not a word). I hear the words "drifter" and "camper" and my elbow immediately flies behind my head and I start humming the *Deliverance* theme song in my head.

If you're at a point in your life where you've got to be a little crazy, try at least to be a little safe, too—like letting someone know when you're drifting out for a rendezvous. Thanks!

Lovingly&logically yours,
Laurie

—twelve—

Life After Ex:

The Care and Feeding of Your New Pet Boyfriend

Like a new pet, new boyfriends require special attention when transitioning to a new home. It's important to make the introduction as smooth and hassle-free as possible. For best results, follow these simple steps when bringing any new pet boyfriend home.

Have a place for him to sleep that's all his own.

A new pet boyfriend is territorial. While somewhere in the back of his primitive mind he senses others have come before him, he does not want or need to be reminded of this. Remove all traces of previous pets prior to bedding down.

Set the stage with polite indifference.

While scheduled feedings, play time, and rest are ultimately controlled by you, your new pet boyfriend needs to feel as if he's free. Initially, pretend you don't much care where he goes or what he does. You'll be surprised how quickly he checks in with you for direction and guidance. Before you know it, this big puppy will be nothing but a lap dog.

The first time a new pet boyfriend makes a mess in the house, let it go.

In these early stages, allow for criticism-free bonding. Remember, everything is new for the little critter! He's doing the best he can; routine is his nature—change is not. There will be plenty of time for administering corrective behavior as he settles in and grows dependent.

New pet boyfriends do not always arrive well-groomed.

Instill good habits early! Take your pet shopping while he's still interested in pleasing you. Later, as resistance builds and compliance wanes, you may resort to other behavioral methods such as withholding "treats" and enforcing "time-outs."

Generally, new pet boyfriends are eager to please. Early missteps can often be traced to poor training with previous owners or early trauma with the pack bitch. So with a little luck, a lot of love, and proper care and feeding, your new pet boyfriend will be chasing, fetching, sitting up, and begging for more in no time. He (and you!) will be the envy of the neighborhood!

Sense of Self

Girls,
one's internal
sense of self
should not be
dictated by
whether or not
you have a man
in your life...

It's much more important
he be in your bed,
don't you think?

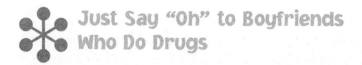

Just Say "Oh" to Boyfriends Who Do Drugs

Dear Laurie,

I am dating someone who I have been with for almost a year and a half. Just recently, I found out that he has been doing harsh drugs. Not only is he doing them, but he is selling them. We got into a huge fight and he promised to quit everything. I don't know if I should call it quits after putting all this time and effort into making our relation-ship work. I don't know if I can/should trust his word that he will quit or if I should just break it off. Please help.

Sincerely, Confused

Dear "Confused,"

I'm confused—you've been dating a guy who's lied to you about drug use and you're wondering if he's trustworthy? If you were:

   A. born yesterday, the answer is a resounding, "Yes, you can trust this guy 110 percent,"or

   B. born the day before yesterday or earlier, read on.

If "promising to quit everything" were so easy, Betty Ford would be so broke and out of work it wouldn't even be funny and her clinic would've been converted to condos decades ago. What drugs are *you* on?!?!!? I understand you love and have invested much with this coke-snootin,' pot-tokin,' heroin-smokin' galumph of a guy, so that's where we shall begin, 'kay?

I'm always one for assuming the worst-case scenario, so let's assume it together. You've been dating this guy for eighteen months, only recently to find he's not only doing but dealing drugs. (Pause here: there's actually some merit in that—he believes enough in the product he's selling to use it himself. That's like using a testimonial, a very respected tactic in the advertising world, by the way.) Let's assume he's been doing this since you met him. Zip it—no lip—just assume it, dammit! We're worst-casing here. But there are other things about this guy that have made the last year and a half worthwhile (place tweety-bird sounds here). Okay. Is it worth giving him a chance before you dump his sorry ass? Yes, and I'll tell you why:

1. It's what you want to hear. If it wasn't what you wanted to hear, you would've kicked his questionably trustworthy butt to high heaven the minute you found out and you wouldn't be writing in to me, a veritable stranger.

2. Maybe he is the one case in a million, the exception that allows us to make rules, that freak of nature who can turn his act around on a dime and parlay his drug-selling skills into more legitimate work like...consulting.

3. You did what you did because love came to town....

First off, this guy must seek counseling and a good support group for waste-oids wouldn't hurt either. He must stop hanging out "wit de boys" or whatever skank element he's been dealing with—you see that advice offered in all the after-school specials on bad-seed kids (and even if all his "clients" are those pseudo-upstanding, white-collar, drug-user-types, they still qualify as skanks). It's also very important that you be clear on what behavior changes you need to see and in what time frame, so you're not sitting around and rotating, waiting for this potentially chronic ne'er-do-well to come around. Got it?

The short answer: Be afraid. Be very afraid or at least be very cautious because squeaky clean, non-drug-user-types like yourself don't understand the allure of the almighty mind-altering arena. Remember: actions speak louder than words. If his actions don't start speaking volumes pronto and you still stay with him, well, then you'll just have to write in again for another tongue-lashing about why you have no self-esteem and are wasting your life on a loser. Until then.

Lovingly&logically yours,
Laurie

Short, Balding, Semi-Attractive Male Molds Woman into Jell-o Jiggler

Dear Laurie

My situation is this...I am a relatively attractive woman. I have been seeing a short, balding, semi-attractive male for about five months now. Well, whenever I'm near him, I'm like jiggling Jell-O. To make a long story short, I have questioned him about the state of our relationship (i.e. are we friends? more? etc.). The answer I get is, "I like hanging out with you."

My question to you is this...should I cut off all sexual relations with him until I get an answer or what should I do to get an answer from him??

Desperate for an Answer in Wisconsin

Dearest "Desperate (for an answer) in Wisconsin,"

Notice the fine use of the parentheses? I put them there for a reason because not only do I believe you are Desperate for an Answer, I think you are just plain Desperate. Per usual, the answer lies within your very own question. You have given us so many plump and juicy clues. So, without further ado, "Pat, I'm ready to solve the puzzle."

Paragraph Two, Line One:

"My question to you is this...should I cut off all sexual relations with him until I get an answer or what should I do to get an answer from him??"

Paragraph One, Line Four:

Pay close attention to the distinct phrasing, "...the answer I get is 'I like hanging out with you.'" (See that? "...the answer I get is..." By God, she asks a question and gets an answer. It's like magic, I tell you. Magic!)

"Desperate," look at me. Over here. I'm talking to you. What don't you understand about his answer? Short, balding, semi-attractive male has spoken. He has told you he enjoys tennis, fishing, and the fact that you're available for back-to-back rounds of "hide the salami" and "thankyouverymuch now go get me a beer."

Sounds to me like you don't care for short, balding, semi-attractive male's answer, but you asked and boyfriend—I mean screw-pal—answered. Unfortunately, Desperate-in-Cheeseland, when we ask questions, we do get to formulate the questions, but we do not get to dictate the answers.

Harsh! Harsh! Harsh! all of you are saying. I'm even saying it, which is why I'm now taking this station break.

Jell-O Jiggler, we've all been there (chorus: Oh, honey, don't you know we have?). And when you travel the rocky road to true love (chorus: Which, by the way, you are not yet on), you gots to take the balder with the better. And so, during this time of temporary sexual detour (chorus: How good can it be if you describe him as the evolutionary equivalent of a preverbal Woody Allen?), get what you need and move on! Because, girlfriend, the two of you are not only not more than friends, you don't seem to be friends at all (remember: friends don't let friends drive short, balding, semi-attractive men home).

And one more thing—what is up with you pointing out that you are more attractive than this guy because you sure do make a point of it (as have I)? I get the feeling you can't believe a guy you find less-than-your-physical ideal is blowing you, I mean not blowing you, I mean blowing you off (there, whew!). I think you're more attracted to him because he's blowing you, I mean not blowing you, oh, forget it. That's a dangerous trap—wanting someone simply because they don't want you. Then again, I may be blowing, I mean not blowing, no, I really do mean blowing smoke out of my ass.

The short, balding, semi-attractive answer: "Desperate"? Are you still reading this? If you want more from this short, balding, semi-attractive male, you need to do your jiggling elsewhere. Think a little more about what you really want from a relationship and then go after it—girlfriends should not settle for anything less.

Lovingly&logically yours,
Laurie

The
End

thirteen

What to Expect When You're Least Expecting:

A Counterintuitive Commitment to One's Singlehood

a s anyone will tell you, love happens when you least expect it. The concept is akin to walking backward into the future—who gets it? It's a Zen state you half aspire to and half say, "Screw it," over while downing a stirred—not shaken—martini.

Ninety-nine point nine percent of the single, female population is expecting. To not expect is to be without hope and to be without hope, well, we know where that leads (to worm eating, see the Introduction). Let's just agree that whoever made up the concept of "least expectance" was either high on crack or a professional sadomasochist. Expecting that someday soon a hunk-a-chunk-a-burnin'-love will fall from the sky into your martini glass is human nature, so congrats on being human.

In case you think you might be part of the .1 percent of the population who is "not expecting," take this simple quiz to find out:

Answer "yes" or "no" to the following five questions

1. Do you expect to answer this question correctly?

___ yes ___ no

2. Do you expect the sun will come out tomorrow, tomorrow?

___ yes ___ no

3. Do you expect to get your money back for this book because this quiz is so lame?

___ yes ___ no

4. Do you expect you will keel over and die some day?

___ yes ___ no

5. Have you read *Great Expectations*?

___ yes ___ no

If you answered "yes" to any of the above questions, you're expecting! So get over your bad self and join the crowd.

So, you're expecting—big whoop! Question is, what to do in the meantime? Interpretive dance? Vulcan mind-meld? How about that "Mother" tattoo you've always wanted? Well, all that and more.

Find joy! That's right. Find joy within your expecting self. I'm not talking about skipping around and smiling like a circus idiot. I mean discovering things that have real meaning for you and then doing them. Finding joy and enjoyment makes the current relationship you are in—the one with yourself—a contented one. Yes, you read right. You are in a relationship with yourself.

And if you can't have a good relationship with yourself, how can you expect to have a good one with somebody else? It's like trying to get out a permanent stain—doesn't happen. Being content with yourself exponentially increases your chances of finding joy with another. Why? Because contented people look and smell delicious. Like freshly baked bread, you're naturally drawn to them.

Does all this seem a bit touchy-feely? A little cosmic, perhaps? Yeah, whatever. Bottom line is:

❋ Get off your skinny/fat (circle one) ass;

❋ Start on something you've always wanted to do (or learn about);

❋ Aspire to the theory of "least expectance";

❋ Be good to yourself;

❋ Have another martini.

About the Author

Published author and humorist, Laurie Frankel, feels her pain (and figures everyone else should, too!) and expertly expresses it with edge, humor and poignancy. When not penning grocery store haiku or telling it like it is, this former east coast gal can be found whooping it up in southern California. Join the fun and email her by visiting her online love column Laurie's LoveLogic at www.laurieslovelogic.com.